DEVELOPING LANGUAGE SKILLS:
Writing 2

Frameworks for Writing

Peter Dougill

English Adviser, West Sussex County Council

Sue Hackman

Teacher of English, Queen Mary's College, Basingstoke

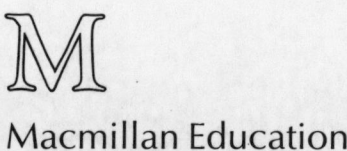

Macmillan Education

First published 1987

Published by
MACMILLAN EDUCATION LTD
Houndmills, Basingstoke, Hampshire RG21 2XS
and London
Companies and representatives
throughout the world

Designed by Linda Reed
Illustrated by Sue Lisansky and Illustra Design
Printed in Hong Kong

British Library Cataloguing in Publication Data
Dougill, Peter
Frameworks for Writing.—
(Developing language skills. Writing; 2)
1. English language—Composition and
exercises
I. Title II. Hackman, Sue   III. Series
808'.402   PE1408
ISBN 0–333–40819–5

Contents

Acknowledgements

Thanks are due to the students and English Department staff at Imberhorne School, East Grinstead between 1977 and 1983.

The authors and publishers wish to thank the following who have kindly given permission for the use of copyright material:

Jonathan Cape Ltd for extracts from *How are Verses Made?* by V. Mayakovsky, trans. G. M. Hyde. Faber and Faber Ltd. for 'In a Station of the Metro' and 'Ts'ai Chi'h' from *Collected Shorter Poems* by E. Pound; extracts from *Lord of the Flies* and *Pincher Martin* by W. Golding; and 'Phone-Call Night-Time' by Michael Rosen from the play *Backbone*. Donald Hall for his poem 'Reclining Figure' from *The Alligator Bride Poems*, Harper and Row (1969). Heinemann Books for extract from *The Jewel in the Crown* by P. Scott. Michael Joseph Ltd for extract from *There is a Happy Land* by K. Waterhouse. Macmillan London Ltd for extract from *George, Don't Do That* by J. Grenfell. New Directions Publishing Corporation for 'Children's Games' from *Pictures from Brueghel* by William Carlos Williams, copyright © 1962 W. Carlos Williams. Harold Ober Associates Inc. for extract 'You should have seen the mess' from *Collected Stories* by M. Spark, © 1958 Copyright Administration Ltd. Penguin Books Ltd. for extracts from *The Citadel of Chaos* by S. Jackson, © 1983 S. Jackson. Routledge & Kegan Paul PLC for extracts from *The Book of Nasty Legends* by P. Smith. The Society of Authors on behalf of the Bernard Shaw Estate for extract from *Pygmalion* by G. B. Shaw. Tavistock Publications for extracts from *Knots* by R. D. Laing.

The authors and publishers wish to acknowledge the following illustrative sources:

Not Now Bernard by David McKee, reproduced by kind permission of Andersen Press Ltd, p. 59. *Angry Arthur* by H. Oram and S. Kitamure, reproduced by kind permission of Andersen Press Ltd, pp. 64 and 65. Used with permission of the Automobile Association, from the *AA Book of Country Walks* p. 2 Daymer Bay, pp. 44 and 45. *AA Complete Atlas*, p. 54. By kind permission of the Trustees of The British Library, Ms. no. Add 38510 folio 234, Dickens, p. 83; Ms. no. 3038 folio 1, Austen, p. 84; Ms. no. Add 4808 folios 81–2, Pope, p. 85; Ms. no. 46700 folio 18, Carroll, p. 89; Ms. no. 851 folio 128b, Chaucer, p. 90. *Dinner at Alberta's* by Russell Hoban, illustrated by James Marshall, reproduced by kind permission of Jonathan Cape Ltd (illustration) and David Higham Associates Ltd (text), pp. 62 and 63. Chad Valley Co. Ltd, pp. 35, 36. *Albert and the Green Bottle* by Elizabeth and Gerald Rose, reproduced by kind permission of Faber and Faber Ltd, pp. 60 and 61 (top). Hallmark Cards Inc., p. 7. By kind permission of the Trustees of W. Heath Robinson, p. 41. *Gorilla* by A. Browne, reproduced by kind permission of Julia MacRae Books, copyright 1983 Anthony Browne, pp. 60 and 61 (bottom). Mansell Collection, pp. 1, 13. Museum of Modern Art, New York, Henry Moore Collection, *Reclining Figure II* 1960 (given in memory of G. David Thompson), p. 15. Museum of Modern Act, New York, Vincent van Gogh Collection, *The Starry Night* 1889 (acquired through the Lillie P. Bliss Bequest), p. 16. *The Reader's Digest Repair Manual* p. 593, used with permission, p. 39. The Reader's Digest Association Ltd London: the illustrations are taken from *The New Illustrated Guide to Gardening* p. 171, Pineapple, used with permission, p. 40.

The publishers have made every effort to trace the copyright holders, but where they have failed to do so they will be pleased to make the necessary arrangements at the first opportunity.

Preface

The suggestions for writing that this book provides have all been tried and tested in the classroom, and have grown out of work with a cross-section of students in comprehensive schools and FE colleges. Essentially, they have all proved themselves as enjoyable tasks, which have helped the students concerned to progress as independent writers.

This book was then compiled with GCSE firmly in mind. It aims to fulfil the National Criteria's demands for content as applied to the 'writing' domain:

> Opportunities must be provided to develop a variety of styles of writing in what may be termed 'closed' situations (e.g. the writing of letters, reports and instructions) where the subject matter, form, audience and purpose are largely 'given' and in what may be termed 'open' situations (e.g. narrative writing and imaginative/personal response to a range of stimuli and experience) where such factors are largely determined by the writer. Response to reading may include the opportunity to write factually or imaginatively in developing and exploring themes and ideas arising from what is read.

In more detail, the Assessment Objectives are fulfilled as shown in the grid by each of the writing assignments:

1 To understand and convey information;
2 To understand, order and present facts, ideas and opinions;
3 To evaluate information in reading material and in other media, and select what is relevant to specific purposes;
4 To articulate experience and express what is felt and what is imagined;
5 To recognise implicit meaning and attitudes;
6 To show a sense of audience and an awareness of style in both formal and informal situations.

The whole range of assignments therefore provides a variety of 'closed' and 'open' contexts as well as a combination of short and extended pieces of work.

We believe most firmly that writing is not just about the finished product, the piece of work that's handed in to the teacher, but also about the process, the things that go on in your mind while you are composing your work. We believe that the writing process is a thinking process. We hope that some of the strategies and opportunities suggested here will help you to become a better writer, not just in your English lessons but also in other subjects, and in your outside life as well.

	1	2	3	4	5	6
1 Pictures in your mind						
Read and draw	√	√	√			√
Greetings cards					√	√
The amazing valentine				√		√
The dream journey				√	√	
Pictures and poems				√	√	√
2 Points of view						
My earliest memories				√	√	√
Myself	√	√	√	√	√	√
Monologue		√		√	√	√
Knots				√	√	
Writing in role		√		√	√	√
Telling and showing		√		√	√	√
3 Writing in context						
Rules to a board game	√	√				√
Estate agents' blurbs	√	√	√		√	√
Instructions	√	√				
School/college brochure	√	√			√	√
Home town	√	√	√			√
Country walk	√	√				√
4 Choosing a medium						
The Great Steamboat Race	√	√	√			√
Phone-call Night-time	√	√	√		√	√
The campaign		√	√			√
Imaginary planet		√				√
Poetry and prose				√		√
5 Making stories						
An illustrated children's story				√		√
Modern myths	√	√	√		√	√
Do-it-yourself stories	√			√		√
The citadel				√		√
Story openings			√		√	√
Letter sequence	√	√		√		√
6 The writing process						
Reading journal		√		√	√	
Critical diary		√		√	√	
Personal research	√	√	√	√		√

1 Pictures in your mind

Close your eyes and think of . . . a stretch of coastline.
- Picture it in detail.
- Explore it in your mind for two or three minutes.
- Now try it with words. Catch your picture in words, collecting together ideas and phrases which come to mind, then work on them until you have a few sentences.

Now try it with
- a cold place
- a distant world
- a view through a broken window
- a face
- a stranger's home

Now jot down any words or phrases suggested by these faces:

Details from *Portrait of Himself and Saskia* and *Self-Portrait*, both by Rembrandt

Write a sentence for each one and ask a friend to match the sentence to the right face.

Now picture this:

In a station of the metro

The apparition of these faces in a crowd;
Petals on a wet, black bough.

EZRA POUND

And this:

Ts'ai chi'h

The petals fall in the fountain,
    the orange-coloured rose-leaves,
Their ochre clings to the stone.

EZRA POUND

We have tried to convey two thoughts with this introduction:
first, that to visualise something clearly in your mind will help
you to write about it perceptively and accurately; and secondly,
that the best professional writers, especially poets, 'think
visually' before they put pen to paper.
    This section gives you 'picture starters' to help your writing.

Read and draw

This activity encourages you to read closely and to create
pictures in your mind as you read. Readers who have these
mental images will become more involved and understand more
from their reading. You will also gain the skill of selecting and
using written information by putting it into other forms, such as a
sketch or a diagram. Your own writing should improve in clarity
and detail if you try to bring vivid pictures into the minds of your
readers.
    Read these passages and then follow the instructions.

from: Lord of the Flies

Read

They were on the lip of a cirque, or a half-cirque, in the side of the
mountain. This was filled with a blue flower, a rock plant of some
sort; and the overflow hung down the vent and spilled lavishly
among the canopy of the forest. The air was thick with butterflies,

lifting, fluttering, settling.

Beyond the cirque was the square top of the mountain and soon they were standing on it.

They had guessed before that this was an island: clambering among the pink rocks, with the sea on either side, and the crystal heights of air, they had known by some instinct that the sea lay on every side. But there seemed something more fitting in leaving the last word till they stood on the top, and could see a circular horizon of water.

Ralph turned to the others.

'This belongs to us.'

It was roughly boat-shaped: humped near this end with behind them the jumbled descent to the shore. On either side rocks, cliffs, tree-tops and a steep slope: forward there, the length of the boat, a tamer descent, tree-clad, with hints of pink: and then the jungly flat of the island, dense green, but drawn at the end to a pink tail. There, where the island petered out in water, was another island; a rock, almost detached, standing like a fort, facing them across the green with one bold, pink bastion.

The boys surveyed all this, then looked out to sea. They were high up and the afternoon had advanced; the view was not robbed of sharpness by mirage.

'That's a reef. A coral reef. I've seen pictures like that.'

The reef enclosed more than one side of the island, lying perhaps a mile out and parallel to what they now thought of as their beach. The coral was scribbled in the sea as though a giant had bent down to reproduce the shape of the island in a flowing, chalk line but tired before he had finished. Inside was peacock water, rocks and weed showing as in an aquarium; outside was the dark blue of the sea. The tide was running so that long streaks of foam tailed away from the reef and for a moment they felt that the boat was moving steadily astern.

Jack pointed down.

'That's where we landed.'

Beyond falls and cliffs there was a gash visible in the trees; there were the splintered trunks and then the drag, leaving only a fringe of palm between the scar and the sea. There, too, jutting into the lagoon, was the platform, with insect-like figures moving near it.

Ralph sketched a twining line from the bald spot on which they stood down a slope, a gully, through flowers, round and down to the rock where the scar started.

'That's the quickest way back.'

WILLIAM GOLDING

Draw Sketch and label a map of the island.

Reflect The boys are stranded. They have no idea where they are or how they are going to survive. From your reading and sketching, can you begin to answer these problems?

Read

from: Robinson Crusoe

Had any one in England been to meet such a man as I was, it must either have frighted them, or raised a great deal of laughter; and as I frequently stood still to look at my self, I could not but smile at the notion of my travelling through Yorkshire with such an equipage, and in such a dress. Be pleased to take a sketch of my figure, as follows.

I had a great high shapeless cap, made of a goat's skin, with a flap hanging down behind, as well to keep the sun from me as to shoot the rain off from running into my neck; nothing being so hurtful in these climates as the rain upon the flesh under the cloaths.

I had a short jacket of goat-skin, the skirts coming down to about the middle of my thighs, and a pair of open-kneed breeches of the same; the breeches were made of the skin of an old he-goat, whose hair hung down such a length on either side that like pantaloons it reached to the middle of my legs; stockings and shoes I had none, but had made me a pair of somethings, I scarce know what to call them, like buskins, to flap over my legs and lace on either side like spatter-dashes; but of a most barbarous shape, as indeed were all the rest of my cloaths.

I had on a broad felt of goat's-skin dry'd, which I drew together with two thongs of the same, instead of buckles, and in a kind of a frog on either side of this, instead of a sword and a dagger, hung a little saw and a hatchet, one on one side, one on the other. I had another belt not so broad, and fastened in the same manner, which hung over my shoulder; and at the end of it, under my left arm, hung two pouches, both made of goat's-skin too; in one of which hung my powder, in the other my shot. At my back I carry'd my basket, on my shoulder my gun, and over my head a great clumsy ugly goat-skin umbrella, but which, after all, was the most necessary thing I had about me, next to my gun. As for my face, the colour of it was really not so moletta-like as one might expect from a man not at all careful of it, and living within nine or ten degrees of the equinox. My beard I had once suffered to grow till it was about a quarter of a yard long; but as I had both scissars and razors sufficient, I had cut it pretty short, except what grew on my upper lip.

DANIEL DEFOE

Draw

Sketch Robinson Crusoe.

Reflect

He has been shipwrecked on his island for many years. From your reading and sketching, can you suggest some of the ways he has managed to survive?

Read

from: Pygmalion

Next day at 11 a.m. Higgins's laboratory in Wimpole Street. It is a room on the first floor, looking on the street, and was meant for the drawing room. The double doors are in the middle of the back wall; and persons entering find in the corner to their right two tall file cabinets at right angles to one another against the walls. In this corner stands a flat writing-table, on which are a phonograph, a laryngoscope, a row of tiny organ pipes with a bellows, a set of lamp chimneys for singing flames with burners attached to a gas plug in the wall by an indiarubber tube, several tuning-forks of different sizes, a life-size image of half a human head, shewing in section the vocal organs, and a box containing a supply of wax cylinders for the phonograph.

Further down the room, on the same side, is a fireplace, with a comfortable leather-covered easy-chair at the side of the hearth nearest the door, and a coal-scuttle. There is a clock on the mantelpiece. Between the fireplace and the phonograph table is a stand for newspapers.

On the other side of the central door, to the left of the visitor, is a cabinet of shallow drawers. On it is a telephone and the telephone directory. The corner beyond, and most of the side wall, is occupied by a grand piano, with the keyboard at the end furthest from the door, and a bench for the player extending the full length of the keyboard. On the piano is a dessert dish heaped with fruit and sweets, mostly chocolates.

The middle of the room is clear. Besides the easy-chair, the piano bench, and two chairs at the phonograph table, there is one stray chair. It stands near the fireplace. On the walls, engravings: mostly Piranesis and mezzotint portraits. No paintings.

GEORGE BERNARD SHAW

Draw

Draw a labelled floor-plan of the stage described here, or sketch the view from the front row of the auditorium.

Reflect

Before the action begins, the audience look at the set, and what conclusions do they draw? Discuss the value of the set.

Read

from: The Jewel in the Crown

Going from the cantonment bazaar which is still the fashionable shopping centre of Mayapore, along the Mahatma Gandhi road, once styled Victoria road, the traveller will pass the main police barracks on his left and then, on his right, the Court house and the adjacent cluster of buildings, well shaded by trees, that comprised, still comprise, the headquarters of the district administration. Close by, but only to be glimpsed through the gateway in a high stucco wall, similarly shaded, is the bungalow once known as the chummery where three or four of Mr. White's unmarried sub-divisional officers – usually Indians of the uncovenanted provincial civil service – used to live when not on tour in their own allotted areas of the district. Beyond the chummery, on both sides of the road, there are other bungalows whose style and look of spaciousness mark them also as relics of the British days, the biggest being that in which Mr. Poulson, assistant commissioner and joint magistrate, lived with Mrs. Poulson. Almost opposite the Poulsons' old place is the bungalow of the District Superintendent of Police. A quarter of a mile farther on, the Mahatma Gandhi road meets the south-eastern angle of the large square open space known as the *maidan*, whose velvety short-cropped grass is green during and after the rains but brown at this season. If you continue in a northerly direction, along Hospital road, you come eventually to the Mayapore General Hospital and the Greenlawns nursing home. If you turn left, that is to say west, and travel along Club road you arrive eventually at the Gymkhana. Both the club and hospital buildings can be seen distantly from the T-junction of the old Victoria, Hospital and Club roads. And it is along Club road, facing the *maidan*, that the bungalow of the Deputy Commissioner is still to be found, in walled, arboreal seclusion.

PAUL SCOTT

Draw   Draw a street map of the town and label the buildings.

Reflect   What can you tell about the history of the town from this description?

Write   Now try writing a passage of your own, from which a friend could make a sketch. The result will soon tell you how effective your writing is in communicating your mental images. Try:
■ a floor-plan of your home, or bedroom
■ your route home from school
■ your family tree

Greetings cards

This activity will give you a chance to use your imagination and powers of design and presentation. Greetings cards require a visual appeal to complement their verbal messages. You are invited to look carefully at this very familiar and traditional form of greeting, identifying its main features and using them for yourself.

Discuss

Millions of greetings cards are sent each year. Collect as many different types as possible and sort them into categories.

In a small group, discuss how the design and content of each category fits its purpose and audience.

Write

Now, invent a new festival or celebration (eg. 'Pets' Day' or 'Failure') and design a card for it, with an appropriate message.

The amazing valentine

In this activity, you bring an unexpected visual element to your writing by expressing it in an unconventional shape or format, adding an immediate visual meaning to the work. This is an opportunity to stretch your powers of wit, ingenuity and presentation.

Read

Here, for example, is a valentine message. Start at the arrow and get to the heart in the middle.

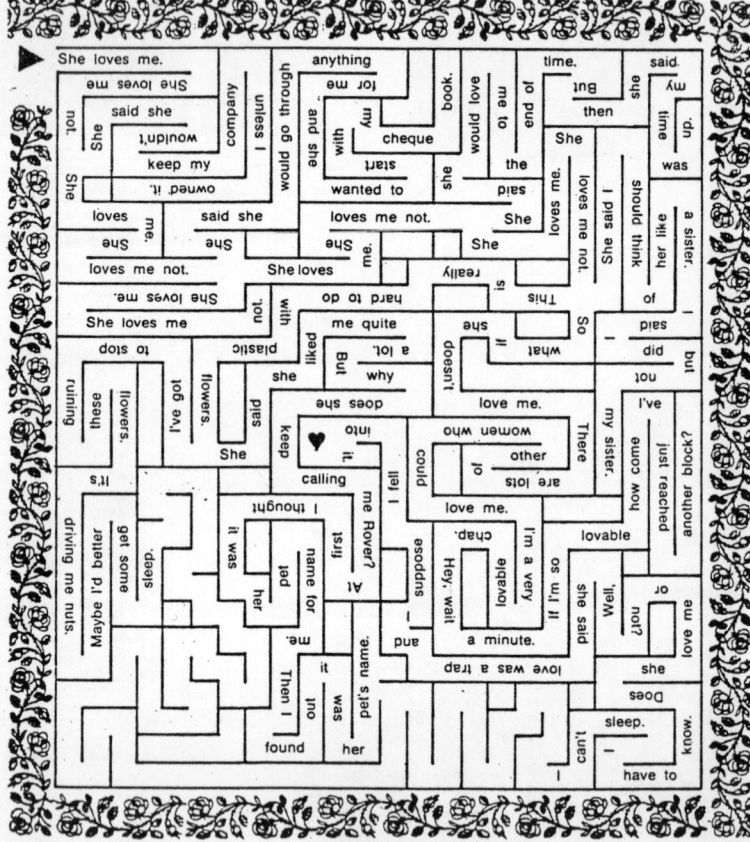

Write

Take a message or an idea, and find an appropriate but unusual form in which to express it. Some ideas for you to try:
- Lost!
- You won't believe this excuse, but . . .
- Caught in the one-way system
- Flow diagram or board game entitled *Life* or *School*

Further reading

If you enjoy this kind of thing, your teacher will tell you where to find concrete poems, which are similar.

The dream journey

This activity calls for imagination: the making of images. You are asked to raise pictures in your mind's eye and write down what you see there. No two people have quite the same images: the angle, mood, detail and significance are quite special to you. This writing will exercise your capacity to make and refine your own mental images.

Write

This is a sort of game. The idea is that each image says something about you. It stands for something in your life.

Imagine this. You are walking down a path. Do you see a picture in your mind's eye? What sort of path is it? Wide? Narrow? Winding? Steep? Rocky? What is on either side? What is the landscape?
   Write a paragraph describing the path.

Imagine this. You are walking along the path when you see an object glinting in the sun on the ground before you. Stooping to pick it up, you realise it is a key. What sort of key is it? And is it shiny? Rusty? Gold? Silver? Heavy or delicate?
   Write a paragraph describing this key and say what you do with it.

You continue walking but find the path blocked by water, which you must cross. This water might be a river, a puddle, a lake . . . whatever comes to mind first. How do you imagine crossing it? You can create, if you like, anything to help – stepping stones, bridge, boat – whatever appeals.

Write a paragraph describing the water and your crossing of it.

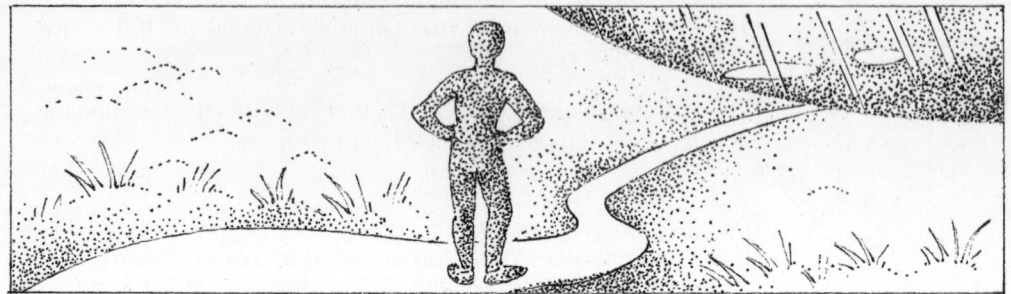

As you walk on, you pass a particular tree which catches your attention.

Describe this tree.

You continue your journey. Ahead is a bend in the path, around which you cannot see. As you approach it, someone you don't know appears walking in the opposite direction. What is your first reaction?

Describe your approach to the bend, the appearance of the stranger and your reaction.

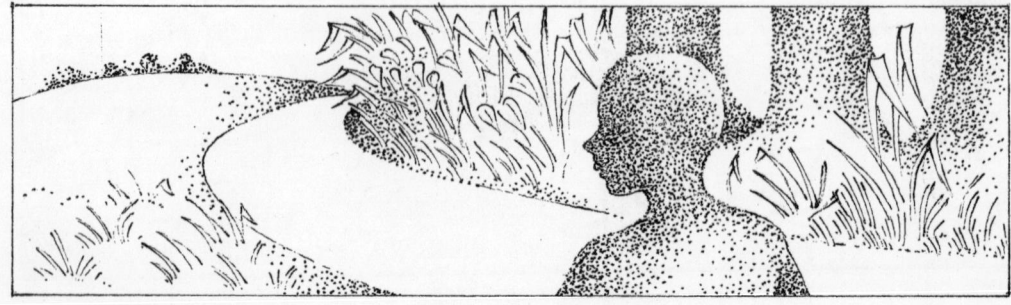

You walk on. Some time later, you come across a small cottage which attracts you. At first you think you will walk by, but something makes you pause, and pushing open the gate, you approach the place. You think you will just peep in through the window, so you go up to it, and looking in, you see . . . what?
Write what you see.

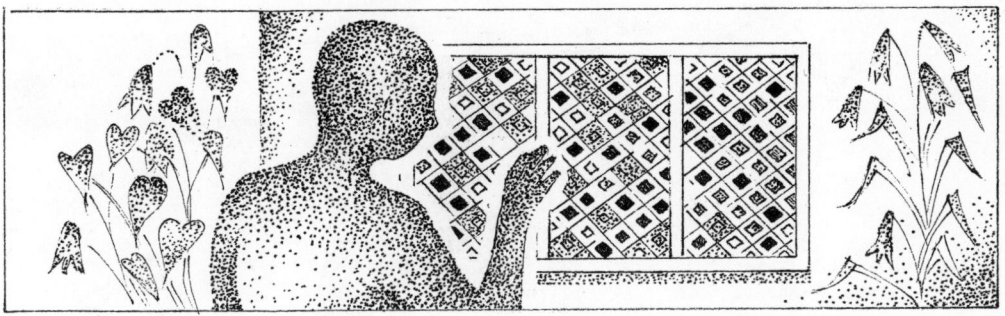

Some time later, you are walking along the path when you find an obstruction in your way. What is this obstruction and how do you overcome it?

Further along, by the side of the path you encounter a strange garden, enclosed within a square wall. You look over into the garden.
Write a paragraph describing the garden.

The path ends at a wall. As far as the eye can see, this wall has no end.

Describe the wall, and if you can see beyond it, what is there? If you cannot see beyond it, what do you hope would be there?

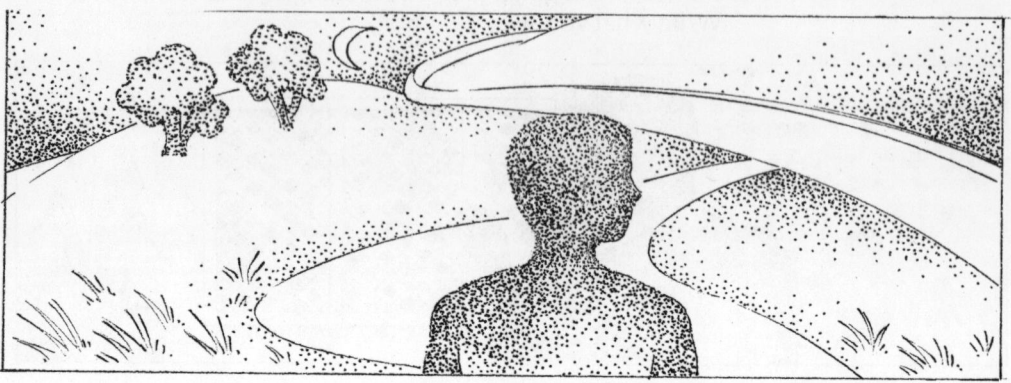

Reflect

On page 18 you will find information which will help you to 'read' your images. There are no final interpretations – it is, after all, just a game – but you will realise that images sometimes echo feelings we have inside us.

Some people like to go back and rework one or two of their best images by editing their first notes and sharpening the details. We have seen some very good poems started this way.

Pictures and poems

A strong visual sense can stimulate your imagination and help you to write with detail, form and feeling. Painters and sculptors work with paint and stone but you work with words. This is an exercise in making sense of images. These are not always visual but can also be verbal: pictures painted with words.

Look

Here is a picture called *Children's Games*. Look carefully and try to make out which games are being played and then list them.

Children's Games, by Breughel

As you build up your list ask yourself what kind of games they are and what kind of players. Note down anything you find interesting or intriguing about the picture.

Read

Then you might like to compare your observations with this poem by William Carlos Williams.

Children's Games

i

This is a schoolyard
crowded
with children

of all ages near a village
on a small stream
meandering by

where some boys
are swimming
bare-ass

or climbing a tree in leaf
everything
is motion

elder women are looking
after the small
fry

a play wedding a
christening
nearby one leans

hollering
into
an empty hogshead

ii

Little girls
whirling their skirts about
until they stand out flat

tops pinwheels
to run in the wind with
or a toy in 3 tiers to spin

with a piece
of twine to make it go
blindman's-buff follow the

leader stilts
high and low tipcat jacks
bowls hanging by the knees

standing on your head
run the gauntlet
a dozen on their backs

feet together kicking
through which a boy must pass
roll the hoop or a

construction
made of bricks
some mason has abandoned

iii

The desperate toys
of children
their

imagination equilibrium
and rocks
which are to be

found
everywhere
and games to drag

the other down
blindfold
to make use of

a swinging
weight
with which

at random
to bash in the
heads about

them
Brueghel saw it all
and with his grim

humor faithfully
recorded
it

WILLIAM CARLOS WILLIAMS

Discuss the picture in the light of the poem.

Write   Try using your notes and jottings to fashion a poem of your own.

Look   Now study the following pictures. Concentrate on them hard for
a few minutes until their shape, feel and detail stay in your mind
when you close your eyes.
   Picture each work in your mind's eye and jot down on a piece
of paper any words, ideas and reactions which jump into your
mind:

Two-Piece Reclining Figure, No. 2, by Henry Moore

Starry Night, by Vincent Van Gogh

Read

When you have finished, compare your reactions with those of two poets who wrote about these works:

Reclining Figure

Then the knee of the wave
turned to stone.

By the cliff of her flank
I anchored,

in the darkness of harbors
laid-by.

DONALD HALL

The Starry Night

That does not keep me from having a terrible need of – shall I say the word – religion. Then I go out at night to paint the stars.

Vincent Van Gogh *in a letter to his brother*

The town does not exist
except where one black-haired tree slips
up like a drowned woman into the hot sky.
The town is silent. The night boils with eleven stars.
Oh starry starry night! This is how
I want to die.

It moves. They are all alive.
Even the moon bulges in its orange irons
to push children, like a god, from its eye.
The old unseen serpent swallows up the stars.
Oh starry starry night! This is how
I want to die:

into that rushing beast of the night,
sucked up by that great dragon, to split
from my life with no flag,
no belly,
no cry.

ANNE SEXTON

Write

1   Find a picture:
■ an old photograph, perhaps from your family album
■ a picture in a colour-supplement magazine which intrigues
  you
■ a painting you like
■ a postcard
Sit quite still and concentrate on it. Wait for as long as it takes for
the thoughts to start flowing.
2   Keep a clean sheet of paper by your side and jot down any
passing thought, response or idea about the picture until your
page is fairly full.
3   When you feel you have exhausted your thoughts look over
your material and select a handful that you think are interesting
enough to work on.
4   You might like to extend or re-express them by adding new
material that will bind them together into the form of a poem.
5   Put your first draft to one side for a while, maybe until next
lesson, then look at it again. Continue working on the poem until
it satisfies you.

Note on reading 'The dream journey'

Reading your images can be interesting, but remember this is a game, not a psychological test. The images are old ones, embedded in our culture, but they have only general associations. Roughly speaking, they 'read' as follows:

path: the path of your life
key: marriage
water: the female sex, perhaps your mother or guardian
tree: the male sex, perhaps your father or guardian
stranger: strangers; meeting new people, making friends
cottage window: inside yourself; your emotional 'interior'
obstruction: how you deal with obstacles, hazards and problems
    in your life
garden: the romantic, sensual aspect of your nature
wall: death

For example, a narrow, stony, uphill path may suggest a life that is similarly hard going. A shiny elaborate key may suggest a romantic and sentimental view of marriage. Fearful strangers and immense obstacles sometimes imply a fear of the unknown or of challenge.

You might like to discuss the way that myths, dreams and symbols also have meanings outside themselves. Perhaps you know other games like this, which claim to tell you something about your secret self.

2 Points of view

Each person sees the world from his or her own point of view.

And we all carry round with us a set of prejudices, beliefs, habits, expectations and a lifetime of experiences which condition the way we see the world.

In this section of the book, you are asked to think from other points of view than just your own, because no one will be a wholly successful writer if he or she can articulate only his or her *own* point of view. Every novelist, for instance, has to consider a different viewpoint of the world for each different character.

The other side of this coin is that you will have to write for different *audiences*, and if you have thought about the needs and preferences of the people you are writing for, it will help you to choose the most appropriate tone, vocabulary and style.

My earliest memories

Start by exploring very fully your *own* point of view in life. Use your skills in writing to make sense of things which have happened in your own past. Writing is a way of holding on to the past and yet telling it through the eyes of later experience. We tend to remember things that have impressed us, however small they may seem. Writing will preserve your best memories for you, and help you to put the past into perspective.

Write

There is no need to write a full autobiography, though this could grow into one if you enjoy it. Pick a handful of memories that still seem fresh and important to you. Try to identify your very first memory of being alive; it is a very special memory. Collect your memories together.

Here are some starting points which may jog your memory:

■ Christmas presents
■ first day at school
■ getting lost
■ something that frightened you
■ going on holiday
■ the birth of a brother or sister
■ an accident
■ getting in trouble
■ grandparents
■ birthday parties
■ rooms you once knew well
■ moving house
■ nursery, playgroup, childminder
■ family events (weddings, funerals)
■ games you used to play
■ favourite toys
■ your first best friend

Some people like to bring in their old photographs, old toys and other mementoes of their childhood. They can recall memories. Parents will sometimes write or tell you about incidents you have remembered, but from their point of view. Set them some homework.

It is fun to read your memories to other people. Sometimes, talking will remind you of other things you had forgotten. You may want to go back and rework what you have written, or run your memories together into an essay or autobiography.

You might like to collect other people's memories on a theme (eg. 'first day at school'). Older people have memories of the world before you were born and will enjoy passing on their experiences.

Further reading   There are many interesting autobiographies you might enjoy reading. Here are some which may make you laugh:

There is a Happy Land by Keith Waterhouse
Ash on a Young Man's Sleeve by Dannie Abse
My Oedipus Complex by Frank O'Connor
Cider with Rosie by Laurie Lee

Here are some extracts we have enjoyed:

from: *Ash on a Young Man's Sleeve*

Saturday mornings, I used to climb into my mother's bed and lie between my parents and ask questions:
   'Who made the world?'
   'God.'
   'Who made God?'
   When Mam would go and prepare breakfast I would lie on the warm part where she had been. My father snored with his mouth ajar. His face was turned towards me and I could see the individual pores in the skin over his nose, clearly. His skin was like a used dartboard. He opened one eye fishily and saw me upside down. 'What are you looking at?' he said sleepily. 'Your nose,' I said. He closed his eyes again. The wallpaper in the bedroom was pinkish, so warm and kindly. He opened his left eye once more. 'What's wrong with my nose?' he asked. 'Nothing,' I said, but he turned over and I gazed at the back of his head. 'You're going bald a bit on the crown,' I remarked. Father grunted but he soon moved again, this time on to his back. 'You have quite a prominent Adam's apple,' I said. 'Be quiet,' he said. 'You have hair growing in your ears,' I continued. He pulled the bedclothes over his head. 'What are you doing that for?' I shouted.

DANNIE ABSE

from: *Unreliable Memoirs*

At home things were a bit easier than at school. Once or twice I announced my intention of running away, but my mother defused the threat by packing me a bag containing peanut-butter sandwiches and pyjamas. The first time I got no further than the top of our street and was back home within the hour. The second time I got all the way to Rocky Point Road, more than two hundred yards from home. I was not allowed to cross Rocky Point Road. But I sat there until sunset. Otherwise I did my escaping symbolically, tunnelling into the poultry farm and surfacing among the chooks with a crumbling cap of birdshit on my head.

The teacher's pet image would have followed me home if my mother had had her way. She had a deadly habit of inviting the neighbours in for tea so that she could casually refer to my school reports a couple of hundred times. The most favoured recipient of these proud tirades was Nola Huthnance, who lived four doors down. Nola Huthnance was no mean talker herself, being joint holder, with her next-door neighbour Gail Thorpe, of the local record for yapping across the back fence – an unbeatable lunch-to-sunset epic during which there was no point at which one or the other was not talking and very few moments when both were not talking simultaneously. But not even Nola Huthnance could hold her own when my mother got going on the subject of her wonderful son and his outstanding intelligence.

CLIVE JAMES

from: There is a Happy Land

'Have we to talk in Arjy Parjy?' said Ted.

Arjy Parjy was like a secret language we had in our class. You had to put 'arj' in the middle of every word, and if you could speak it fast you were right good.

'Darjo yarjou sparjeak Arjy Parjy?' I said.

'Yarjes. Darjo yarjou?'

We walked back up the road as far as the furniture van and shouted to the woman in the armchair: 'Darjo yarjou sparjeak Arjy Parjy?' She shouted: 'Wait till I go down to that school! You'll be laughing on the other side of your faces!' We shouted: 'Couldn't catch a copper!' and crossed over the road, seeing how straight we could go walking backwards.

'Carjan yarjou sparjeak Arjy Parjy as warjell as marjee?' said Ted.

'Yarjes, I carjan sparjeak it barjetter tharjan anybarjony,' I said.

'*I-i-it* isn't anybarjony. I mean, it arjisn't anybarjony,' said Ted. 'It's anybarjody.'

'*Said* anybarjody.'

'Yarjou darjidn't.'

'Darjid.'

'Darjidn't.'

'Darjid.'

We walked on past the branch library, just before you get to our street. Ted puts his hands to his mouth and bawls out: 'Got any books to give away?' and it echoed back at us.

'Smashed windows, by Eva Brick,' I said.
'What a smell, by Hoo Flung Dung,' said Ted.
'A walk in the woods, by Theresa Green.'
'No, this is it. A walk in the woods by Theresa Brown.'
'No. A walk in the woods by Theresa Tall.'
'Walk in the woods by Theresa Smelly.'
'Warjalk in the warjoods by Theresa Smarjelly.'

KEITH WATERHOUSE

Myself

Now progress to looking at yourself through other people's eyes, and present their views in relevant forms. This activity asks for a great deal of honesty and some careful thought about which style is appropriate to which situation.

Write

1   Make a school report slip very like your own. Choose a subject or an overall tutor's report and write a report on yourself. Be honest, accurate and realistic. If you can bear it, look over your last school report for help.

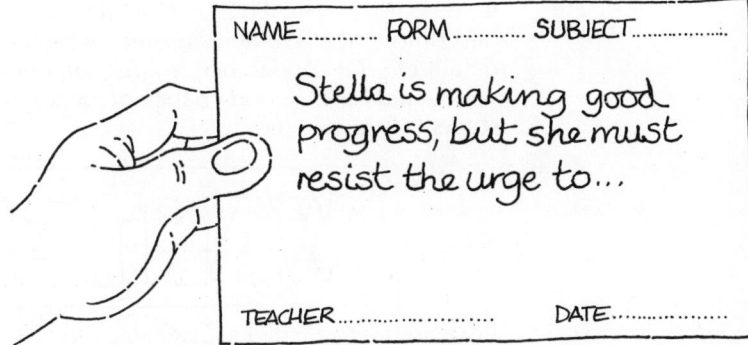

2   An adult who knows you well – maybe a parent or a guardian or an employer – is overheard talking about you on the telephone. How does the speech go?

23

3   Targ is a spider from the planet Mars. He has been sent to
Earth to observe (from his invisible space capsule) one Earthling
for one Earth day. He has never seen Earthlings before today. On
the whole, he finds them to be rather unpleasant, pudgy and
puzzling creatures of strange habits and revolting physical
appearance.

As it happens, you are the Earthling whom Targ has been
observing for the last 24 Earth hours (87 space-ticks in Martian
time).

Write Targ's report on your appearance, activities and
behaviour today.

STAR DATE 20.93.4T.S4. 1109
TARG REPORTING

THE HUMAN SPECIMEN IS A
CREATURE OF PUZZLING
HABITS...

4   This is a physical description of you – perhaps a policeman's
description or a 'Wanted!' poster – which will give accurate
details of your appearance, so that someone who has never met
you would have a good chance of identifying you out of the
students in your class.

WANTED

THE SUSPECT IS APPROXIMATELY
5'4" IN HEIGHT WITH SHOULDER
LENGTH BROWN HAIR...

5 Ask a friend to contribute a statement to your file.

My friend Stella is.........................
.....................wicked sense of
humour..
always in..
.................................and never
does her...
....Sometimes can
be...................... .

SIGNED..A. Friend..............

6 One of your possessions wishes to say a few words about you. If your school bag could talk, or your bedroom or your comb . . . or any one of your belongings . . . what would it say?

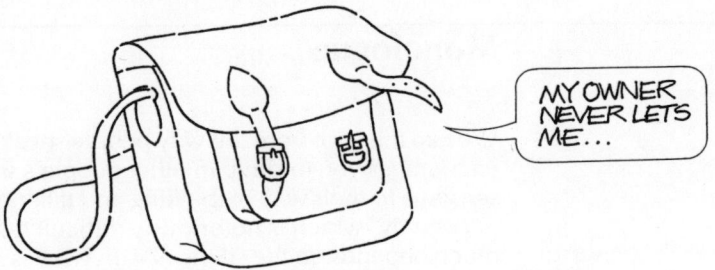

7 Your pet wishes to make a brief statement about you. Translate your pet's woofs, barks, miaows, hisses or tweets into English.

8 And you – what do you have to say on the subject of yourself?

Monologue

We can tell a lot from the way people speak. This activity encourages you to stand in other people's shoes and become sensitive to their way of thinking and talking. It is also an exercise in comedy, which is notoriously difficult to write. Notice how much depends on the silences – on what is *not* said – and how much the reader is involved in working out their meaning.

Read

A monologue means one person speaking. In this case we guess there are others present and interrupting, but the one voice of the primary-school teacher conveys the whole scene:

from: George, Don't Do That

[*It is winter*]
Children – it's time to go home, so finish tidying up and put on your hats and coats. Some of our mummies are here for us, so hurry up.
   Billy won't be long, Mrs Binton. He's on hamster duty.
   Now let's see if we can't all help each other.
   Janey – I said help each other. Help Bobbie carry that chair, don't pin him against the wall with it.

We're having a go at our good-neighbour policy here, Mrs Binton, but it doesn't always . . .

Neville, off the floor, please. Don't lie there.

And Sidney, stop painting, please.

Because it's time to go home.

Well, you shouldn't have started another picture, should you. What is it this time?

Another blue man! Oh, I see, so it is.

All right, you can make it just a little bit bluer, but only one more brushful, please, Sidney.

Neville, I said get up off the floor.

Who shot you dead?

David did? Well, I don't suppose he meant to. He may have meant to then, but he doesn't mean it now, and anyhow I say you can get up.

No, don't go and shoot David dead, because it's time to go home.

George. What did I tell you not to do? Well, don't do it.

And Sidney, don't wave that paint-brush about like that, you'll splash somebody. LOOK OUT, DOLORES!

Sidney! . . . It's all right, Dolores, you aren't hurt, you're just surprised. It was only a nice soft brush. But you'd better go and wash your face before you go home.

Because it's all blue.

Sidney, I saw you deliberately put that paint-brush up Dolores's little nostril.

No, it wasn't a jolly good shot. It was . . . I don't want to discuss it, Sidney.

Now go and tell Dolores you're sorry.

Yes, now.

Thank you, Hazel, for putting the chairs straight for me.

You are a great helper.

Thank you.

And thank you, Dicky, for closing the cupboard door for me.

Dicky, is there somebody *in* the cupboard?

Well, let her out at once.

Are you all right, Peggy? What did you go into the cupboard for?

But we don't have mices – I mean mouses – in our toy cupboard. Mouses only go where there is food, and we don't have any food in our toy cupboard.

When did you hid a bicky in there?

Every day!

JOYCE GRENFELL

Write

Now you try writing a monologue. Here are some ideas:
- a teacher
- a parent with a young child
- a driving instructor
- someone having difficulties making a telephone call

Knots

It is surprising to realise that we all experience events in different ways: even our closest relationships are open to interpretation. This activity asks you to explore in writing these individual viewpoints. It also encourages you to use writing as a way of 'thinking through' personal experience, making explicit what is implied. As you read, you will need to fill out the text in your imagination and put this into writing.

Read

The extracts which follow show a breakdown of communication in a family. Each person has a different view of events. When they tell a third person about them, their misunderstandings are revealed.

Debbie

Debbie's Mum and Dad think	Debbie says
Debbie is happy.	She is very depressed and confused.
She is cheerful and outgoing.	She puts on a show.
There is no tension or friction in the family.	She feels very angry and resentful and feels she cannot talk to her parents about anything.
They are not possessive.	They are. They are always talking about being let down and only want her to do things they want.
Debbie does not go out with boys. She doesn't like going to discos. She doesn't smoke or drink. }	She does.
She likes school.	School bores her.

R. D. Laing has reduced these breakdowns in communication to their most basic forms. He calls them 'knots'. They are a form of vicious circle. Here are some examples of his 'knots':

from: Knots

They are playing a game. They are playing at not
playing a game. If I show them I see they are, I
shall break the rules and they will punish me.
I must play their game, of not seeing I see the game.

Jill thinks
  Jack thinks
    Jill does not see something.

```
Jack does think
   Jill sees it
but Jack does not see
   Jill thinks
   Jack thinks
   Jill does not see.
```

JILL   You think I am stupid

JACK   I don't think you're stupid

JILL   I must be stupid to think you think I'm
      stupid if you don't: or you must be lying.
      I am stupid every way:
      to think I'm stupid, if I am stupid
      to think I'm stupid, if I'm not stupid
      to think you think I'm stupid, if you don't.

JILL   I'm ridiculous

JACK   No, you are not

JILL   I'm ridiculous to feel ridiculous when I'm not.
      You must
         be laughing at me
      for feeling you are laughing at me
         if you are not laughing at me.

Write

- Choose one of the examples and try to reconstruct the series of events or story from which it comes. Write a play script or a story which reveals the full story behind the 'knot'.
- Now try reading *Phone-call Night-time* (pages 51–3) and try making up your own 'knot' of the problems revealed in the play.
- You might now like to try composing 'knots' based on your own experience.

Writing in role

This is an exercise in reading between the lines, seeing through to the speaker beyond. Woven into the writing are hints and clues about the narrator which we must put together for ourselves. When it is your turn to write, you must think yourself into another life. Be that other person, showing how you think and behave in the way you express yourself. Notice that *how* we say things can reveal more than *what* we say.

Read

In a group, read the following passages.

from: *You Should Have Seen the Mess*

I am now more than glad that I did not pass into the Grammar School five years ago, although it was a disappointment at the time. I was always good at English, but not so good at the other subjects!!

I am glad that I went to the Secondary Modern School, because it was only constructed the year before. Therefore, it was much more hygienic than the Grammar School. The Secondary Modern was light and airy, and the walls were painted with a bright, washable, gloss. One day, I was sent over to the Grammar School with a note for one of the teachers, and you should have seen the mess! The corridors were dusty, and I saw dust on the window ledges, which were chipped. I saw into one of the classrooms. It was very untidy in there.

I am also glad that I did not go to the Grammar School, because of what it does to one's habits. This may appear to be a strange remark, at first sight. It is a good thing to have an education behind you, and I do not believe in ignorance, but I have had certain experiences, with educated people, since going out into the world.

I am seventeen years of age, and left school two years ago last month. I had my A certificate for typing, so got my first job, as a junior, in a solicitor's office. Mum was pleased at this, and Dad said it was a first-class start, as it was an old-established firm. I must say that when I went for the interview I was surprised at the windows, and the stairs up to the offices were also far from clean. There was a little waiting room, where some of the elements were missing from the gas fire, and the carpet on the floor was worn. However, Mr. Heygate's office, into which I was shown for the interview, was better. The furniture was old, but it was polished, and there was a good carpet, I will say that. The glass of the bookcase was very clean.

I was to start on the Monday, so along I went. They took me to the general office, where there were two senior shorthand-typists, and a clerk, Mr. Gresham, who was far from smart in appearance. You should have seen the mess!! There was no floor covering whatsoever, and so dusty everywhere. There were shelves all round the room, with old box files on them. The box files were falling to pieces, and all the old papers inside them were crumpled. The worst shock of all was the tea cups. It was my duty to make tea, mornings and afternoons. Miss Bewlay showed me where everything was kept. It was kept in an old orange box, and the cups were all cracked. There were not enough saucers to go round, etc. I will not go into the facilities, but they were also far from hygienic. After three days, I told Mum, and she was upset, most of all about the cracked cups. We never keep a cracked cup, but throw it out, because those cracks can harbour germs. So Mum gave me my own cup to take to the office.

Then at the end of the week, when I got my salary, Mr. Heygate said, 'Well, Lorna, what are you going to do with your first pay?' I did not like him saying this, and I nearly passed a comment, but I said, 'I don't know.' He said, 'What do you do in the evenings, Lorna? Do you watch Telly?' I did take this as an insult, because we call it TV, and his remark made me out to be uneducated. I just stood, and did not answer, and he looked surprised. Next day, Saturday, I told Mum and Dad about the facilities, and we decided I should not go back to that job. Also, the desks in the general office were rickety. Dad was indignant, because Mr. Heygate's concern was flourishing, and he had letters after his name.

Everyone admires our flat, because Mum keeps it spotless, and Dad keeps doing things to it. He has done it up all over, and got permission from the Council to re-modernise the kitchen. I well recall the Health Visitor remarking to Mum, 'You could eat off your floor, Mrs. Merrifield.' It is true that you could eat your lunch off Mum's floors, and any hour of the day or night you will find every corner spick and span.

Next, I was sent by the agency to a Publisher's for an interview, because of being good at English. One look was enough!! My next interview was a success, and I am still at Low's Chemical Co. It is a modern block, with a quarter of an hour rest period, morning and afternoon. Mr. Marwood is very smart in appearance. He is well spoken, although he has not got a university education behind him. There is special lighting over the desks, and the typewriters are latest models.

MURIEL SPARK

from: *The Sound and the Fury*

Through the fence, between the curling flower spaces, I could see them hitting. They were coming toward where the flag was and I went along the fence. Luster was hunting in the grass by the flower tree. They took the flag out, and they were hitting. Then they put the flag back and they went to the table, and he hit and the other hit. Then they went on, and I went along the fence. Luster came away from the flower tree and we went along the fence and they stopped and we stopped and I looked through the fence while Luster was hunting in the grass.

'Here, caddie.' He hit. They went away across the pasture. I held to the fence and watched them going away.

'Listen at you, now.' Luster said. 'Ain't you something, thirty-three years old, going on that way. After I done went all the way to town to buy you that cake. Hush up that moaning. Ain't you going to help me find that quarter so I can go to the show tonight.'

They were hitting little, across the pasture. I went back along the fence to where the flag was. It flapped on the bright grass and the trees.

WILLIAM FAULKNER

Reflect   Discuss your impressions of the narrator. Look closely at the
language and discuss the exact words and phrases which gave
you these impressions.

Write   Now try your hand at writing in role. Here are some ideas:
- a very small child visiting a dentist or a fairground for the first
time
- someone bitter, irritable or grumpy
- a pet speaks out
- someone feeling uncomfortable in his or her, surroundings
- 'My view of the earthlings', by a visitor from outer space

Telling and showing

This is another exercise in writing from different points of view.
The same event can be seen quite differently, depending on
where you stand. It can be described differently, too, so that the
reader shares your perspective.

Read   Read these two passages.

from: *Robinson Crusoe*

Nothing can describe the confusion of thought which I felt when I
sunk into the water; for tho' I swam very well, yet I could not
deliver my self from the waves so as to draw breath, till that wave
having driven me, or rather carried me a vast way on towards the
shore, and having spent it self, went back, and left me upon the
land almost dry, but half dead with the water I took in. I had so
much presence of mind as well as breath left, that seeing my self
nearer the main land than I expected, I got upon my feet, and
endeavoured to make on towards the land as fast as I could,
before another wave should return, and take me up again. But I
soon found it was impossible to avoid it; for I saw the sea come
after me as high as a great hill, and as furious as an enemy which
I had no means or strength to contend with; my business was to
hold my breath, and raise my self upon the water, if I could; and
so by swimming to preserve my breathing, and pilot my self
towards the shore, if possible; my greatest concern now being,
that the sea, as it would carry me a great way towards the shore
when it came on, might not carry me back again with it when it
gave back towards the sea.

The wave that came upon me again, buried me at once 20 or 30
foot deep in its own body; and I could feel my self carried with a
mighty force and swiftness towards the shore a very great way;
but I held my breath, and assisted my self to swim still forward
with all my might.

DANIEL DEFOE

from: Pincher Martin

He was struggling in every direction, he was the centre of the writhing and kicking knot of his own body. There was no up or down, no light and no air. He felt his mouth open of itself and the shrieked word burst out,

'Help!'

When the air had gone with the shriek, water came in to fill its place – burning water, hard in the throat and mouth as stones that hurt. He hutched his body towards the place where air had been but now it was gone and there was nothing but black, choking welter. His body let loose its panic and his mouth strained open till the hinges of his jaw hurt. Water thrust in, down, without mercy. Air came with it for a moment so that he fought in what might have been the right direction. But water reclaimed him and spun so that knowledge of where the air might be was erased completely. Turbines were screaming in his ears and green sparks flew out from the centre like tracer. There was a piston engine too, racing out of gear and making the whole universe shake. Then for a moment there was air like a cold mask against his face and he bit into it. Air and water mixed, dragged down into his body like gravel. Muscles, nerves and blood, struggling lungs, a machine in the head, they worked for one moment in an ancient pattern. The lumps of hard water jerked in the gullet, the lips came together and parted, the tongue arched, the brain lit a neon track.

'Moth——'

WILLIAM GOLDING

Reflect

Where were you when you pictured these two men?

Most people see the first man from a distance, as though through a camera. Most people see the second man at close quarters.

Look closely at the passages, and discuss how the writers have got us to look at each man from a certain perspective.

Write

Now try writing about an event from two different perspectives. For example:

- a person reliving a car accident *and*
- the formal police report of the accident

- what happened when your roof fell in *and*
- the architect's report on the roofing defect at property 356/B

- a true experience which upset or excited you (write as 'I') *and*
- the same experience seen from 'the outside', as though it happened to someone else (call yourself by your first name)

3 Writing in context

It is actually much easier to write when you are told the *purpose*, the *audience* and the appropriate *medium*. Most writing you will do in your working life is done with a knowledge of all three. So here is some practice in writing as an estate agent, as a guide and as an instructor, each time working in a specific context.

Rules to a board game

In this activity, you are asked to communicate precise instructions as simply as possible for a future user. Writing rules is a test of accuracy, logic and clarity. You will have to think carefully, missing nothing out, but avoiding confusion and complexity. Your reader must be able to play the game using only the rules you write down. It is therefore important that you look at your writing with a critical eye, anticipating any problems, and being prepared to rewrite as necessary.

Design

Think of all the board games you know. Design and make one of your own. The only way to know if it works is to try it out.

Write

When the game is finished, write a draft of the rules. You might find it useful to look over the rules of board games at home. Some people find it helpful to start off by representing their rules as a flow diagram.

When you have done your best with the rules, hand them over to other students to test by trying them out. They will soon tell you if anything is unclear. They will also be able to tell you how interesting and successful they find the game.

Further reading

There is an interesting collection of old board games in a book called *Play the Game* by Brian Love. You might use it to get ideas.

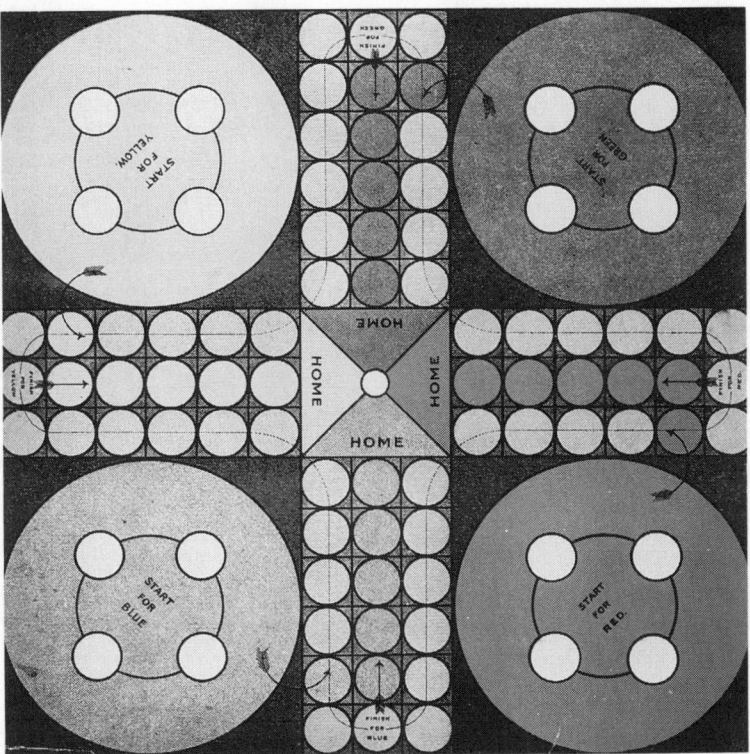

Ludo or Parcheesi

1   This is a game for 2, 3 or 4 players. Each takes 4 counters of the same colour, and places them in the appropriate Starting Enclosure.

2   Players throw the die in turn. A 6 is needed to start, and the successful player then moves 1 counter into the first circle of the track indicated by the arrow. He or she then has another throw, and moves the counter forward by the corresponding number of spaces.

3   At each subsequent throw of a 6, a player may either bring a fresh counter into play, or advance a counter already on the track. A 6 on the first throw always entitles the player to a second turn, but not subsequently, i.e. a third turn is not allowed if another 6 is thrown on the second turn.

4   When a counter is played into a space occupied by an opponent, it takes its place. The displaced counter is returned to its Starting Enclosure from which it is again started in the usual way.

5   When 2 or more counters of the same colour are played into the same space, 1 is placed on top of the other and together they form a Barrier, which no other counter may seize or pass over. If a Barrier prevents a counter being advanced its full number of spaces, that turn is lost.

6   After a counter has been round the outside track and comes back to its own colour, it is played up the centre line of spaces to Home. Here the exact number required must be cast, i.e. the Home mark may not be overshot.

7   The winner is the player who first gets all 4 counters Home.

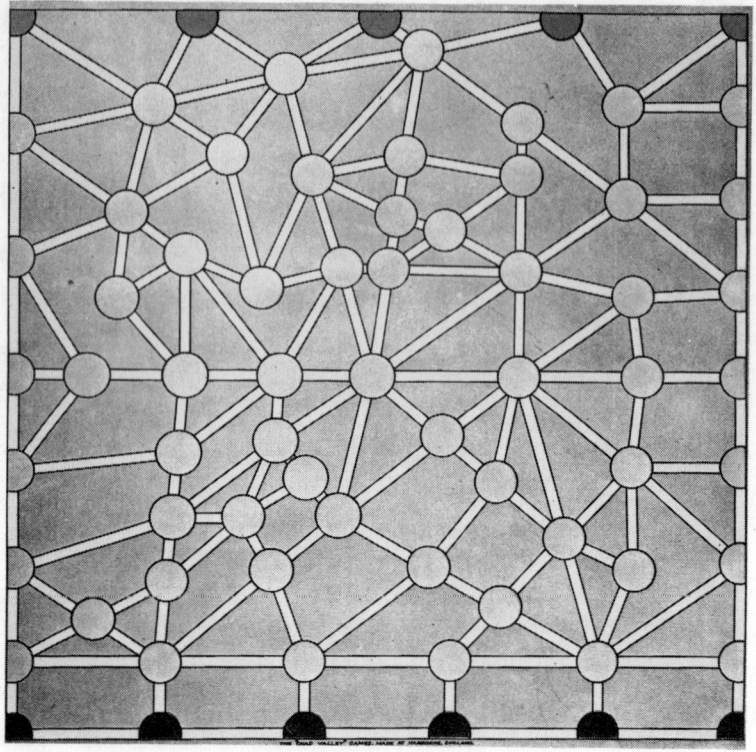

Hare and Hounds

1 This is a game for 2–6 players. One is the Hare, and the other players control the 5 Hounds. The Red counter representing the Hare is placed on the centre spot at the top of the board, and the Blue Hounds occupy any 5 of the spots at the bottom of the board.

2 The object of the game is for the Hare to run past the Hounds and reach Home, which is either of the two centre spots at the bottom of the board.

3 The Hare begins, and may move 1 space at a time in any direction. The Hounds move 1 at a time, and may move in any direction except backwards. The Hounds need not move in rotation but in any order by common agreement.

4 The Hounds cannot 'take' the Hare but can defeat him by hemming him in so that he cannot move.

5 The game is finished either when the Hare reaches Home, or when the Hounds have trapped him so that he cannot move.

Estate agents' blurbs

The point of this activity is to look very closely at the way writing is used to persuade and influence the reader – in this case, to persuade the reader to buy a house. It also gives you an opportunity to write in the same way – to sell a house.

Estate agents sometimes use language in a particular way. They are using language to persuade customers to buy property so that they can earn commission on the deal. On occasions they take great care to choose words that create a pleasing picture in the mind of the client who reads the publicity material. For example, a basement flat could be called a 'garden flat', and a 'compact studio apartment' may really be a small bedsit.

Reflect

Collect several examples of estate agents' publicity handouts. Read and discuss them in a small group.

Write

Make a list of estate agents' terms with realistic definitions alongside. For example:

estate agents' terms	reality
compact studio apartment	small bedsit
garden flat	basement

Write a flattering description of a house you know well, in order to attract a buyer.

You might like to write an alternative version of your description, showing the property in a light you find more honest.

BAXTER PAYNE & LEPPER

Chartered Surveyors
Estate Agents

Established 1760

2 & 4 George Street
Croydon CR9 1ND

01-688 3128

London
Bromley
Beckenham
Orpington
Petts Wood
Biggin Hill

PRICE:
£34,500
FREEHOLD.

AN ATTRACTIVE COTTAGE STYLE PROPERTY IN CONVENIENT AND PLEASANT LOCALITY.

 **BAXTER PAYNE LEPPER**

FEATURES: BUILT JUST AFTER THE TURN OF THE CENTURY OF BRICK UNDER A SLATE ROOF,
THE PROPERTY AFFORDS SPACIOUS ACCOMMODATION WHICH IS IDEAL FOR FIRST TIME PURCHASE.
SOME ESSENTIAL WORKS OF IMPROVEMENT AND RE-DECORATION THROUGHOUT IS NECESSARY.   THE
ACCOMMODATION BRIEFLY COMPRISES *2 BEDROOMS, *BATHROOM AND SEPERATE W.C.,
*SITTING ROOM AND *INTERCOMMUNICATING DINING ROOM, *KITCHEN IN MORE DETAIL AS
FOLLOWS. (All Measurements Are Approximate):

ACCOMMODATION:

GROUND FLOOR:
Entrance Hall: Leading to:
Sitting Room: 13' (Bay) x 8'10" With picture window to front aspect and power
point.
Intercommunicating Dining Room: 11'4" x 9'1" Double power point and glazed
casement door to Rear Garden.
Kitchen: 11'2" x 7'3" Single drainer stainless steel sink unit and range of fitted
wall cupboards, plumbing for washing machine, electric cooker point and power points.
Large cupboard under stairs housing gas meter.

FIRST FLOOR:
Bedroom 1: 12' x 11' With polystyrene tiled ceiling and power point.
Bedroom 2: 10'10" x 6'7" Polystyrene tiled ceiling and power point.
Landing: With built-in hanging cupboard and access trap to roof space.
Bathroom: White modern suite comprising bath and pedestal wash hand basin, Airing
Cupboard housing lagged hot water cylinder and fitted immersion heater.
Seperate w.c:

OUTSIDE:
Gardens: Small front garden and rear garden mainly paved with asbestos and timber
framed garage.
Additional leanto storage area.

RATEABLE VALUE: £211

VIEWING: STRICTLY BY APPOINTMENT WITH OWNERS AGENTS AS ABOVE.

Instructions

This activity asks you to write clear instructions for a future user. You will need to write economically and logically if your reader is to follow them easily and safely.

Read

Look at the instructions for these two operations:

Bicycles Handlebars

Replacing a tape

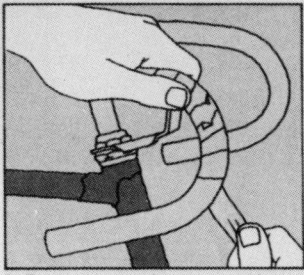

1 Remove attachments such as brake levers from the handlebars and peel off the old tape

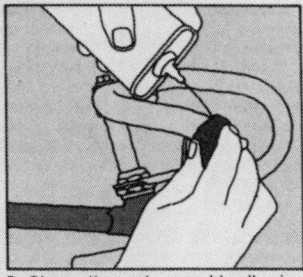

2 Clean dirt and any old adhesive off the handlebars. Petrol is an effective cleaning fluid

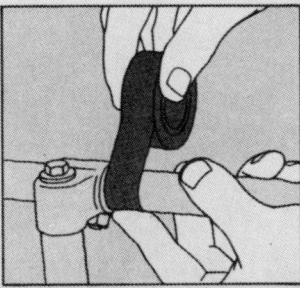

3 Start retaping at the centre of the handlebars—square at first, then at a slight angle to the bar

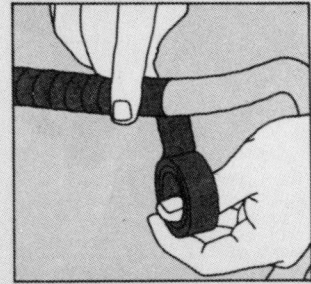

4 Press the tape into place as it is wound. Half cover each coil to get a flat even surface

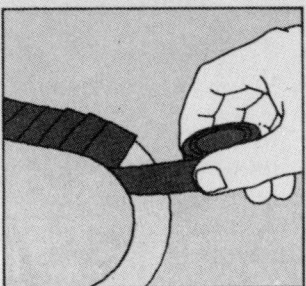

5 Avoid creases and ridged edges when winding round curves, if necessary stretching the tape

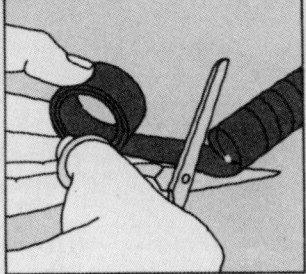

6 Overlap the handlebars by about $\frac{1}{4}$ in. (6 mm). Cut off neatly and tuck the surplus tape inside the tubing

Growing a pineapple plant from a fresh leaf top

Slice the green, leafy top from a fresh pineapple, together with a narrow piece of flesh containing the top row of 'pips' on the skin. Dry off the top for one or two days.

Fill a 3½–4 in. pot to within ¾ in. of its top with moist potting compost; sprinkle a thin layer of coarse sand on top.

Set the pineapple crown on the sand, and sprinkle a little more compost over the fleshy part.

Cover the pot with a polythene bag and put in a shaded position, at a temperature of 18°C (64°F). Rooting generally takes place in about eight weeks, and is indicated by the fresh appearance of the leaf tuft and possibly by new leaves.

Once growth is well established, remove the polythene and repot the plant in a larger pot.

The plant may grow to 2 ft high, but is unlikely to fruit unless given considerable humidity and warmth.

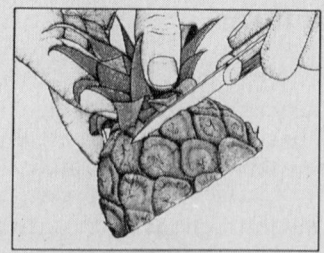

1 *Cut the crown and the top row of 'pips' from a fresh pineapple*

2 *Set the top on a shallow layer of coarse sand sprinkled over compost*

3 *Sprinkle fresh compost over the pineapple and firm with the fingers*

4 *Pull a clear polythene bag over the pot and secure with an elastic band*

Design

Choose an operation or appliance or invent a machine of your own, such as a breakfast-in-bed machine, an apple-picking machine or a dog-exercising machine like the one here.

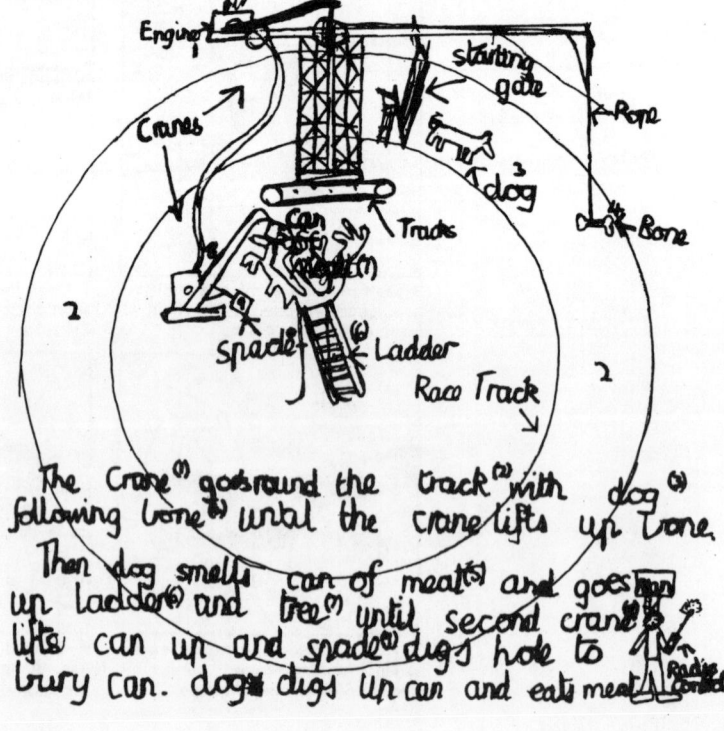

The Dog-Exercising Machine, by Edward de Bono

Six-tier communal cradle, by W. Heath Robinson

Write   Produce your own booklet of instructions, suitable for public use. It is difficult to write clear instructions which a reader can follow alone, so you might have to test out your instructions on a partner or in a group.

School/college brochure

This activity asks you to write informatively and persuasively about your own school or college for the benefit of new students. In it, you must present factual material in a form which is clear, fair and attractive. The tone and type of information must be tailored for your particular readers: students like yourself.

Most large businesses, organisations and institutions produce a brochure which aims to inform readers about the kind of services and amenities that are on offer.

Colleges and universities, for example, send out glossy brochures to persuade young people that they will find being a student at their particular institution enjoyable, lively, varied and stimulating.

School brochures aim to do a similar job. They are usually directed at parents who are thinking of sending their children to a particular school and aim to present an attractive and reassuring picture. However, this picture does not always match the experiences of the students when they arrive!

Write

Your brief is to produce an informative and honest brochure aimed at the students who will be arriving soon at your school or college. You might start by making a list of the items you would want to include.

Home town

In this activity we are asking you to step back from a place you know very well and represent it for a particular audience. Try to keep in mind that your readers won't know your home town so you must select the information that is most interesting and relevant, and that will meet the approval of the editor.

Think

Consider your home town or locality.

You know a lot about it.

Sometimes outsiders want to know about the place you live – in guide books, history books, geography books, atlases, tourist brochures and so on. It is up to you to select what is relevant and to present the information as clearly and interestingly as possible.

Write

Write a short entry about your home town or locality for:
■ a history book, which will include details of the way of life and the significant events of the past
■ a geography book, which will include entries about the location, natural advantages, economy and development of the place
■ a tourist guide, which will direct visitors to the most interesting and picturesque features of your locality
■ any other specialist entries

Country walk

This activity demands clear instructions to be written which will interest as well as inform your readers. It calls for clarity and logic. Be aware that you are writing for the general public.

Many people enjoy walking around places of natural beauty and guides are published to direct tourists around the loveliest parts of the country. A good guide will be interesting, lively, and easy to follow; it will give clear instructions; it will provide accurate descriptions and make brief comments about points of interest on the way.

Read   Pages 44 and 45 show an example of a guide to a country walk, from *No Through Road: The AA Book of Country Walks*.

Write   Imagine you have been invited to design, illustrate and write a guided walk for the beautiful seaside area around Chumley, a map of which is provided below. Use your imagination to provide a commentary on the points of interest, and be aware of the need to direct your reader with clear, accurate and entertaining writing.

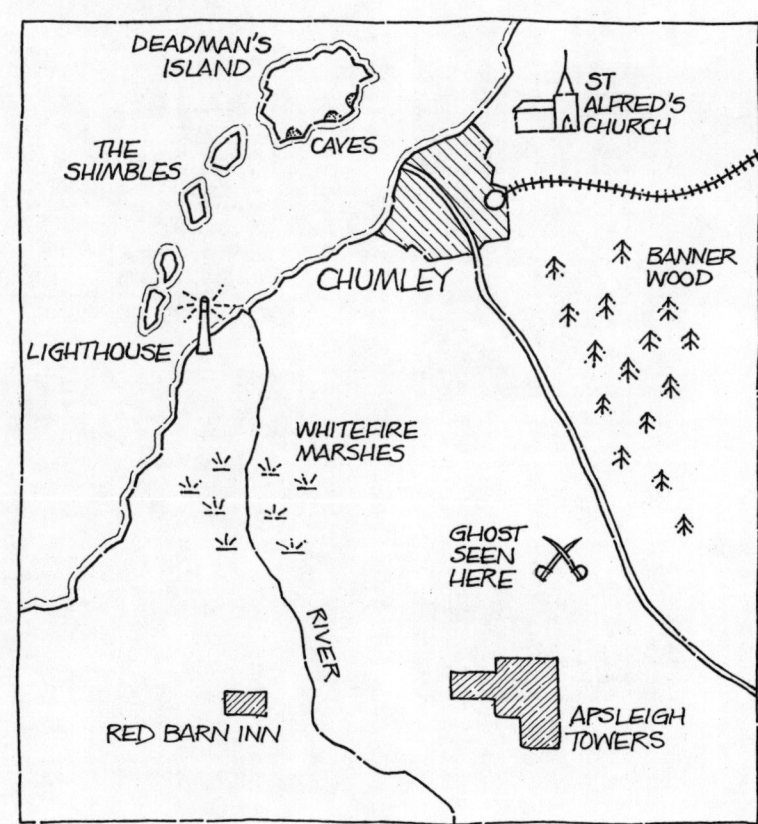

SAND DUNES BY THE CAMEL ESTUARY

Daymer Bay

South-west England

Walk 7

3 miles

A LITTLE NORMAN CHURCH, THREATENED for centuries with burial beneath the shifting sand dunes, is one of the unusual features of this gentle walk on the eastern side of the Camel estuary. If the tide is out, the whole of the return journey can be made along an unbroken expanse of golden sand. The estuary is an important bird-watching area, and the dunes support a wide variety of wild flowers.

CAR PARK At Daymer Bay; or at Rock.

1 From car park turn left, cross stream and walk along top of dunes for 200 yds

2 Turn left and cross golf course to St Enodoc's Church. The footpath is marked with white stones; beware of golf balls

3 From church ascend shallow valley alongside stream, following white stones

4 Cross small footbridge by pond, and bear left up track. Cross tarmac road diagonally, through bushes on to path across golf course, marked by white posts

5 At end of club house drive, turn right down hill to Rock. Turn right at bottom of hill to sea front and quarry car park

6 If tide is out, walk along sands back to Daymer Bay. [If tide in, follow signposted coastal footpath parallel with shore]

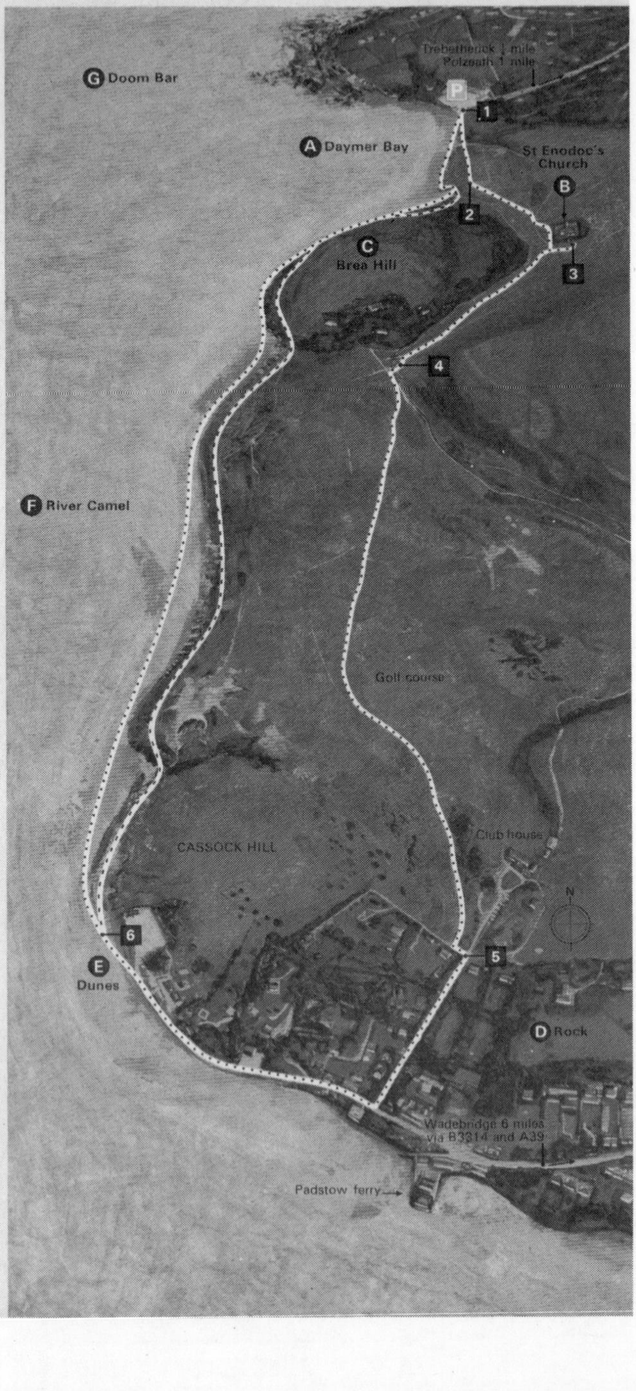

G Doom Bar

A Daymer Bay

St Enodoc's Church

B

C Brea Hill

4

F River Camel

Golf course

Club house

CASSOCK HILL

6

E Dunes

5

D Rock

Wadebridge 6 miles via B3314 and A39

Padstow ferry

WALK 7: DAYMER BAY

Ⓐ Daymer Bay

It was at Daymer Bay that the Welsh missionary St Petroc, Cornwall's patron saint, landed from Ireland during the 6th century, before moving across the estuary to Padstow to establish a monastery. Met by a group of peasants, hot and thirsty from harvesting, the saint made a stream of cool water flow by striking a rock with his staff. The stream across the golf course is said to be St Petroc's stream.

1687 TOMBSTONE IN ST ENODOC'S CHURCH

Ⓑ St Enodoc's Church

St Enodoc's Church dates from Norman times, although the twisted slate spire was added in the 13th century. It is a 'broach' spire – eight-sided, rising from a square tower without a parapet. The church owes its nickname of 'Sinking Neddy' to the fact that several times in the past it has been almost engulfed by shifting sand dunes. In the early 19th century, vicar and congregation were forced to climb down through the roof to hold the annual service required to maintain the church's right to tithes. The building was restored in 1863.

Tamarisk, a Mediterranean shrub, surrounds the churchyard, in which the oldest grave dates back to the 15th century. A coffin rest at least 300 years old stands in the lych-gate, and the stone mortars which line the path to the church door were once used for grinding corn in local houses. Inside the church, the alms box to the left of the door was originally the holy-water stoop; it was found in the north transept when the church was being restored. The font is Norman, standing on a modern granite base. Only the bottom 3 ft of the 15th-century rood screen remains; the rest was crudely cut down when the church was neglected in the early 19th century. The church bell was once the ship's bell of the *Immacolata*, an Italian ship wrecked in 1875 on the rocks on the north side of Daymer Bay.

Ⓒ Brea Hill

The flat green mound of Brea Hill is the site of a Roman settlement. Roman coins, beads and Samian pottery dating from the 3rd and 4th centuries have been found in the neighbourhood.

Ⓓ Rock

Rock is a popular centre for dinghy sailing and there is racing in the estuary during most weeks of the summer. A ferry has been running between Rock and Padstow since 1337; known then as the Black Rock Passage, it gave Rock its name.

The town of Padstow, across the Camel, grew up around St Petroc's monastery and was named Petroc-stow (Padstow) after the saint – although the site had formerly been known as Lode-nek, a Cornish word meaning a fortified inlet. During the Middle Ages, Padstow was a port of some importance, but with the gradual formation of the Doom Bar across the mouth of the estuary its trade declined, and by the middle of the 19th century it had earned the reputation of 'an antiquated, unsavoury fishing town'. The coming of the railway in 1899, however, bringing with it tourists, gave the town a new lease of life. Today it is one of the least commercialised of Cornish resorts. May Day sees Padstow's famous Hobby Horse festival.

Ⓔ Dunes

The marram grass growing on the sand dunes helps to bind them together and prevent the sand shifting. The dunes, because of the high calcium carbonate content of the shell sand, shelter a variety of unusual wild flowers. They include sea holly, sea sand wort, yellow wort and lesser evening primrose.

Ⓕ River Camel

The estuary of the River Camel (*cam-el* is Cornish for 'crooked estuary') is one of the most notable bird-watching sites in the county, particularly for those interested in the winter migrations of waders. Among the waders to be seen are golden plovers, black-tailed godwits, bar-tailed godwits, green sandpipers, wood sandpipers, greenshanks and knots. The Camel and its mouth also provide excellent fishing for bass, mackerel and pollack.

Ⓖ Doom Bar

In the days of sail, the rocky coast of north Cornwall was particularly feared by seamen, as it lacked a safe harbour where vessels could find refuge in rough weather. Padstow, near the mouth of the Camel, seemed to provide an ideal haven, but was in fact a trap for the unwary, for it was guarded by the notorious Doom Bar. This sandbank, covered by a few feet of water, stretched across the mouth of the estuary, leaving only a narrow deep-water channel close under Stepper Point, the western headland at the entrance. Ships seeking shelter found themselves carried by unpredictable winds and currents on to the bar, where many foundered. Today, low tide still reveals this expanse of sand, the graveyard of hundreds of seamen.

PADSTOW: THE WATERFRONT AND CAMEL ESTUARY

4 Choosing a medium

In the last section you worked on purpose, audience and medium in your writing, and these were stated for you each time, as part of the task.

In some circumstances, however, the choice as to which medium is most appropriate for your purpose and your meaning will be *yours*.

In this section you will have the chance to communicate similar ideas in, for instance, a letter, a diary and a report, so that you can observe how each different medium controls and contributes to meaning.

The Great Steamboat Race

This activity asks you to select and organise information for use in a variety of media, presenting it in a way appropriate for each audience. It will help you to get more out of your reading, because the success of the writing will depend on how sensitively you read the passage. Notice how much you read into a story like this: imagination helps you to fill out the characters, events and mood. The ability to 'read yourself into' a story makes you a more effective reader and a more lively writer.

Read

This passage is an account of a steamboat race which caused a sensation in its day. Read the passage carefully before you choose from the writing activities which follow.

The Great Steamboat Race

The greatest race on record – that's how the *New York Herald* described the race up the Mississippi of the steamboats *Robert E. Lee* and *Natchez* in 1870. For more than 1200 miles – from New Orleans to St. Louis – they fought or dodged the current of the most twisting and unmanageable river in the world, while people everywhere hung breathless on the result.

It was not that they were the first to do it. Before the war between North and South other steamboats had raced the same course. But thanks to the new Atlantic cable and that recent invention, the electric telegraph, this race was followed by the whole world almost hour by hour. Everything combined to keep the excitement boiling until the fourth morning. Then a fog came down and nobody – not even the crews – knew what was happening, until one of the boats loomed out of the mist and came storming up to St. Louis, where the thundering cheers told those on board they had won.

At the time Britain was by far the largest owner of sea-going ships in the world, yet the tonnage of all its ships together was less than that of the strange gaudy vessels with big paddle-wheels which glided up and down the lonely Mississippi and its tributaries like swans. Frequently steamboats blew up or caught fire; they seldom lasted more than four years, but often earned their building costs twice over in their first year. Undoubtedly they were the most splendid and exciting things in the lives of all who lived in those parts.

The cottonfields and sugar plantations on which the people lived could not have existed without them, because the river was the only highway, and steamboats were the only things which could go up as well as down it. But they did things for fun and glory as well as for profit.

Before one of them rounded a bend and came into sight of a village the fireman would throw resin on the furnaces so that they could make a dramatic arrival with thick black smoke coiling out of their chimneys. The sight of this and the deep mellow sound of the whistle would send a tingle up the spines of all the small boys in the place. And at night the 'hoooo-hoo-hoo' of a steamboat whistle blowing for a landing, wrote one who heard it as a boy, 'was a sound so filled with mystery and longing that it would hang in your heart like a star'.

After the Civil War ended in 1865, larger and more powerful steamboats were built. One, named after the great Commander of the Southern Army, Robert E. Lee, seemed to be the fastest.

She had the largest high-pressure cylinders ever built in the West and eight large boilers to feed them. She had not taken part in a race, but had broken one or two speed records while going about her normal business, and no other vessel had ever passed her from behind. Then, in 1860, a magnificient newcomer arrived on the scene – the *Natchez*.

She attracted a lot of admiration, and in 1870, after the cotton crop had all been shipped down to New Orleans, she tried out her paces on a run up to St. Louis and broke the record. Only by a little over an hour – but it was a record that had stood for twenty-six years.

Nothing would do now but that she must have a race with the *Lee*. Everyone who lived near the Mississippi was eager for it, and the rival towns where the vessels had been built – Louisville and Cincinnati up the Ohio River – clamoured for it. So a race, from New Orleans to St. Louis, was agreed to, though each Captain put a notice in the local paper to say that he wouldn't dream of such a thing.

The *Lee*, built at Louisville, was 100 yards long. The *Natchez* was a little longer and narrower, which made for more speed. She had bigger paddle-wheels and a particularly sweet shape below the water-line; but her cylinders were smaller. Like the *Lee* she had eight boilers. Her owner-Captain, Thomas Leathers, over-confident, said he would take his usual load of cargo and passengers and make the usual stops.

John Cannon, owner-Captain of the *Lee*, took no cargo and only seventy-five passengers instead of a possible four hundred. He stripped his boat of everything which could be spared.

So the *Lee* was only 4 ft. in the water when the race began, while the *Natchez* was 6 ft. – a handicap which seemed to cancel out any advantage the *Natchez* might have had from her newness and greater length. Cannon also sent upriver a small steamboat, the *Frank Pargoud*, to arrange for coal barges to wait for him in midstream so that he could coal without stopping.

News of the race flashed up the Mississippi and soon excitement was so intense that over a million dollars had been gambled on the result – and thousands more were to be staked right up to the finish. The winner would be entitled to carry a pair of antlers, known as the 'Horns of the Mississippi'. The appointed day for the race was Thursday, 30th June.

At New Orleans thousands of people seething with excitement packed the levee that summer afternoon. Brass bands played – there were a lot of band instruments for sale cheap in the South after the war – and the scent of magnolia was heavy on the air.

Departure was timed for 5.00 p.m., but the *Robert E. Lee*, having her passengers on board and no cargo to wait for, cast off seven minutes early and backed away from the wharf. The four-knot current took her downstream a little way, then, as both paddles smacked into the water, she first stood still and after a few seconds began to move forward. The crowd cheered and a band played 'Hail Columbia!'

Captain Leathers, quite unworried, kept the *Natchez* at the wharf until the last piece of freight was aboard. Someone struck her great bell three times. The engineer replied with three peeps from his whistle, and the pilot took her out after the *Lee*.

Both steamboats hugged the city side of the river to dodge the main current, while the roust-abouts – the Black deckhands – gathered on the low fo'c's'les with twanging banjos to sing their customary parting-songs: 'Sally-go-ral' on the *Lee*, and 'I Ain't Got no Money' on the *Natchez*.

They would sing often during the race – quick songs when they were humping coal on board, and slow songs like 'Alberta, Let Yo' Hair Hang Low' in the evenings, when cabin-passengers would throw money down from the boiler-deck to encourage them. The boats crossed over where the river starts to bend to the south and went out of sight.

Races were timed from St. Mary's Market. The *Lee* passed this at 5.03 p.m. and the *Natchez* at 5.06 p.m. Navigation was easy above New Orleans. The river is a mile wide there. As they belted along high above the flat land shimmering with silvery-green sugar-cane, the *Lee* kept her lead. But after only 30 miles she had to stop and *Natchez* closed the gap. The *Lee*'s 'doctor' had broken down. This was the pump which fed the boilers with water straight from the muddy river, unfiltered, so that one boiler was always out of action being demudded.

They patched it up smartly, but two men had to stay with it for the rest of the run and they had to keep working the bilge-pumps to free the hull from water. Bets made on how far the *Lee* would go in the first hours were lost by this delay. All the same, when the ships turned north at sunset to rush panting through the night, the *Lee* drew ahead again.

A steamboat Captain was an important man who had a bath every day. After his servant had rubbed him down with alcohol and he had changed his linen he would sit on the hurricane deck and drink a mint julep. But once a steamboat was moving under steam the most important man aboard was the Pilot.

A Pilot was paid more than a Captain. His sanctum was the little square pilot-house perched on top of the jumble of cabins and saloons. Here, when the ship was steaming, the Captain could not go. The *Lee* was in the hands of Jesse Jamieson, one of the most famous. He would stand, cigar in mouth and top-hat on head, his fingers a-glitter with rings, at a steering-wheel so big that the lower half was below the deck and out of sight.

The *Lee* was still ahead when they reached Baton Rouge at about 1.30 a.m. Onlookers there could not identify them, however, because of a mist. One was ten minutes and two miles ahead of the other.

The flat open country ended at Baton Rouge. It was thick forest now, with the river wider and shallower and dangerous with trunks rammed end-on into the mud with a spiky end sticking upwards just under the cloudy surface and ready to tear the bottom out of any vessel which ran on to them. Up in the *Lee*'s unlit pilot-house Enoch King, who had taken over the wheel, kept watch for the faint streak on the surface of the water which would tell his expert eye of this danger. The *Natchez* followed.

Next morning the people of Natchez-on-the-hill looked down the river and saw with annoyance that the *Robert E. Lee* was coming upstream more than a mile in front of the ship they were betting on. Their brass band refused to play. A tug was waiting in mid-stream with two coal barges as ordered. The *Lee* slowed, lashed the barges to her as the tug let go, then went ahead again at speed while her roust-abouts shifted the sacks aboard under the urgent and eloquent direction of the mate. Then she cast off the empty barges, and went pounding round the bend.

The *Natchez*, already eight minutes behind, lost another eight minutes by going to the wharf to coal and take on freight. So Captain Leathers had a telegram sent to Memphis, the next coaling-point, to have barges waiting in mid-stream for him too.

The *Lee* led all the second day as they went their winding way to the north through cotton fields. When they reached the town of Vicksburg in the evening the *Natchez* was nearly four miles behind.

And now the two steamboats disappeared from the world for a night and a day into a sinister wilderness where there were no telegraph offices or cheering spectators. This was on the edge of the Yazoo Delta. One can imagine the two pale vessels panting through the night like people in fancy dress who have lost their way coming back from a carnival.

In the early hours of the morning the *Natchez* had the same minor disaster that the *Lee* had had earlier – her supply-pump broke down. They fixed it in thirty-six minutes, but when the waiting world next heard about the race it was that the *Lee* had passed the town of Helena at 4.26 p.m. on Saturday and the *Natchez* was an hour behind.

They reached their next stopping-place, Memphis, late that Saturday night. The *Lee* arrived at 11.15 p.m. and was greeted with fireworks and cannon. The *Natchez* came an hour later, but it was thought she would have an advantage from now on and the betting turned in her favour. Both vessels had broken the record to every place above Baton Rouge so far. There was, however, a disturbing rumour that there was only eight feet of water in the channels above Cairo.

St. Louis was now two hundred miles away. The river was dangerously low. The *Lee* was fifteen miles ahead and going well, but with a defective pump which might yet collapse and put her out of the race. And for both ships there was now a new peril from which the lower river had been free – rocks. Ahead lay a dreaded string of sunken rocks called the Grand Chain, and others beyond it. The bones of more than two hundred steamboats lay strewn along the way to St. Louis. At 8.00 p.m. a thick fog came down and both ships stopped.

The *Natchez* tied up near Devil's Island, eighty miles above Cairo, and waited. The *Lee* stopped for an hour and then went groping on. Along with the coal, she had taken on two pilots at Memphis and they were experts on this part of the river. Captain Cannon could take a chance with these in charge and with his lighter draught.

In the fog the pilot on duty would have to take soundings – a beautiful, eerie business. He would step down to the hurricane deck and strike the big bell. As the deep note floated off into the murk a small boat would be lowered into the water with a lantern in it. As one man rowed ahead, another would throw forward a pipe filled with lead at the end of 33 ft. lint. When the line was vertical he would sing back the depth of water. He had to sing because the pilot couldn't make out one word from another at a distance of perhaps 100 yds, so each depth had a different tune.

As the lantern grew fainter in the distance a rich Black voice would wail back 'M-a-r-k Twain' (12 ft.) or 'Quarter less Ty-r-e-e' (16½ ft.) Worry would come with the cry 'And it's quarter less Twai-nn' (10½ ft.), but comfort with the triumphant 'And it's no-oo Bot-to-om' (over 30 ft.).

Then to the groping *Lee* came another misfortune. The steam-drum which collected steam from the boilers and admitted it to the cylinders began to leak. They stopped the engines, let the pressure down to 90 lb., and rivetted the drum. Gingerly they raised steam again – but only to half-pressure – and went on at reduced speed.

Had the *Natchez* passed them in the meantime? They did not know until they got out of the fog and approached St. Louis. Then the rockets, the cheers, the crowds lining the banks for six miles to the city, the packed windows and housetops told them they had won.

The *Lee*'s time for the journey was three days, eighteen hours, fourteen minutes, against a current averaging five m.p.h. in midstream – three hours and forty-four minutes better than the record run of the *Natchez*. This time has never been beaten. Thirty thousand people were on the wharf. They swarmed over the vessel and almost capsized her. They fixed the Horns of the Mississippi on the pilot house roof, and carried off Captain and Pilots to a civic banquet. The *Lee* had won and songs have been sung about her ever since.

Write

Suggested writing activities:
- Draw and label a map of the race using details in the passage.
- Write a captain's log of the race. (Make your own booklet.)
- Write and lay out the front page of a local newspaper which has covered the progress of the race. Use details from the passage as a starting point.
- Write a letter from either Captain Cannon or Captain Leathers to his family in which he expresses his feelings about the race.
- Imagine there was a local radio station in existence. Using details from the passage, script a special feature programme, including interviews as well as coverage of the facts. You will probably find it helpful to work with a partner or in a group.

Phone-call Night-time

There are a number of activities here which ask you to write in a variety of ways for a number of different purposes, taking into account the reader, the character and conventional styles. This is also an exercise in reading between the lines of a script to work out what is going on, looking at events from different viewpoints to recount them accordingly.

Read

Read this short play in pairs a couple of times. You might like to tape it.

Phone-call Night-time

HARRY　[*excessively ratty*] Hallo.
POLICEMAN　Oh – er – Hallo – Mr Levin? [*pronounced wrongly*]
HARRY　Indeed.
POLICEMAN　Harrow Police Station here, Mr Levin. We've –
HARRY　What the hell do you want?
POLICEMAN　Well I'm sorry to bother you like this but –
HARRY　So am I.
POLICEMAN　Pardon?
HARRY　I said, I'm sorry to be bothered.
POLICEMAN　Well, I'm very sorry, Mr Levin.

HARRY   That's where I came in.

POLICEMAN   Well Sir, this is just a routine enquiry. Well, that is to say we've got a Mr and Mrs Forbes here at the station.

HARRY   You lucky people.

POLICEMAN   I understand that they are anxious about the safety of their daughter.

HARRY   What's the time, for God's sake?

POLICEMAN   Just after half-past two, Sir.

HARRY   Mad – quite mad.

POLICEMAN   She asked us to 'phone you. That is to say the gentleman suggested that we –

HARRY   And what right did she have to do that, pray?

POLICEMAN   Well, Mr Levin – she informed us, rightly or wrongly, as the case may be, that their daughter is in fact reported missing and it is thought that you –

HARRY   Reported missing? Good God, man – as a young lady of twenty-one, as the case happens to be, she chose to accept an invitation to come and stay with us.

POLICEMAN   Is that in fact quite correct, Sir?

HARRY   Quite correct, yes.

POLICEMAN   Well, Sir, the lady – well, the gentleman too I'd say – are very upset and we rather suspected foul play of some sort, Sir.

HARRY   Well, you're wrong. Next.

POLICEMAN   Well, Sir –

HARRY   Yes?

POLICEMAN   Er, could we have a word with the young lady herself, Sir?

HARRY   No.

POLICEMAN   I see, Sir.

HARRY   You probably won't. The aforesaid young lady is in the process of recuperating. She has already slept well over fourteen hours a night for the last week and having been roused myself, I have no intention of disturbing *her* now. Was there anything else?

POLICEMAN   Well, there was one thing I have been asked to ascertain: I wonder could you tell me, Sir, whether the young lady is – er – well, I mean your son *is* there, is he?

HARRY   What's that got to do with you?

POLICEMAN   Well, Sir, I have been instructed to ask whether they – as a couple – well, you know how it is – the lady is very worried.

HARRY   Is she indeed?

POLICEMAN   Well, Sir. Put it like this. They've been here for two hours now and they're driving me round the bend. Can't you give me something to say to them?

HARRY   Ah, well, that's a different story. It's my help you want, is it?

POLICEMAN   Well –

HARRY   No, no, I assure you I sympathise with your predicament. I'd be only too happy to ease some of their weight from off your back so long as I wasn't abetting their mediaeval pryings.

POLICEMAN   Well, look Sir. I would just like to ask – is the lady fit and well, as we do have to make a report – I've got the boss to keep happy as well, you know.

HARRY   Well, write this down in your little report that the lady, Miss Tania Forbes, previously of 'Edenhurst', Laburnum Grove, Godhelpus, Harrow, Middlesex, is twice as happy as she was last week and is now bloody fine. If there was anything else you wanted to know, you can tell your Commanding Officer that I answered the 'phone while still asleep and returned to bed before you were able to complete your routine enquiry. Goodnight. [*Puts down 'phone.*]

POLICEMAN   Goodnight, Sir, and thank . . . [*Puts down 'phone.*]

MICHAEL ROSEN

Reflect

In a group of about four, work out the ten most important questions you would like to ask the writer about *Phone-call Night-time*. Try to find out everything you can about the relationships between the characters mentioned in the play.

Write

Now try writing:
■ The policeman's report of the whole incident. You may make up some of the details, and type your own official form to fill in.
■ A few entries in Tania's diary (or another character's diary). You may like to make a small diary to write in.
■ A letter from Harry's son to Mr and Mrs Forbes, providing your own stationery.

The campaign

This is an exercise in marshalling an argument and projecting it to a wide audience by various means. To enlist their support, you will have to write persuasively, putting forward your case in a logical and accessible manner, applying your arguments where they will have the maximum effect.

Plan

You are the organiser of a campaign about a major piece of development which will destroy a large area of beautiful countryside or places of architectural interest, but which will also bring benefits to the area, such as new jobs.

Create a controversial campaign for your area and decide which side you work for. On page 54, for example, is a map used by students in Sussex who thought up a campaign about a new motorway.

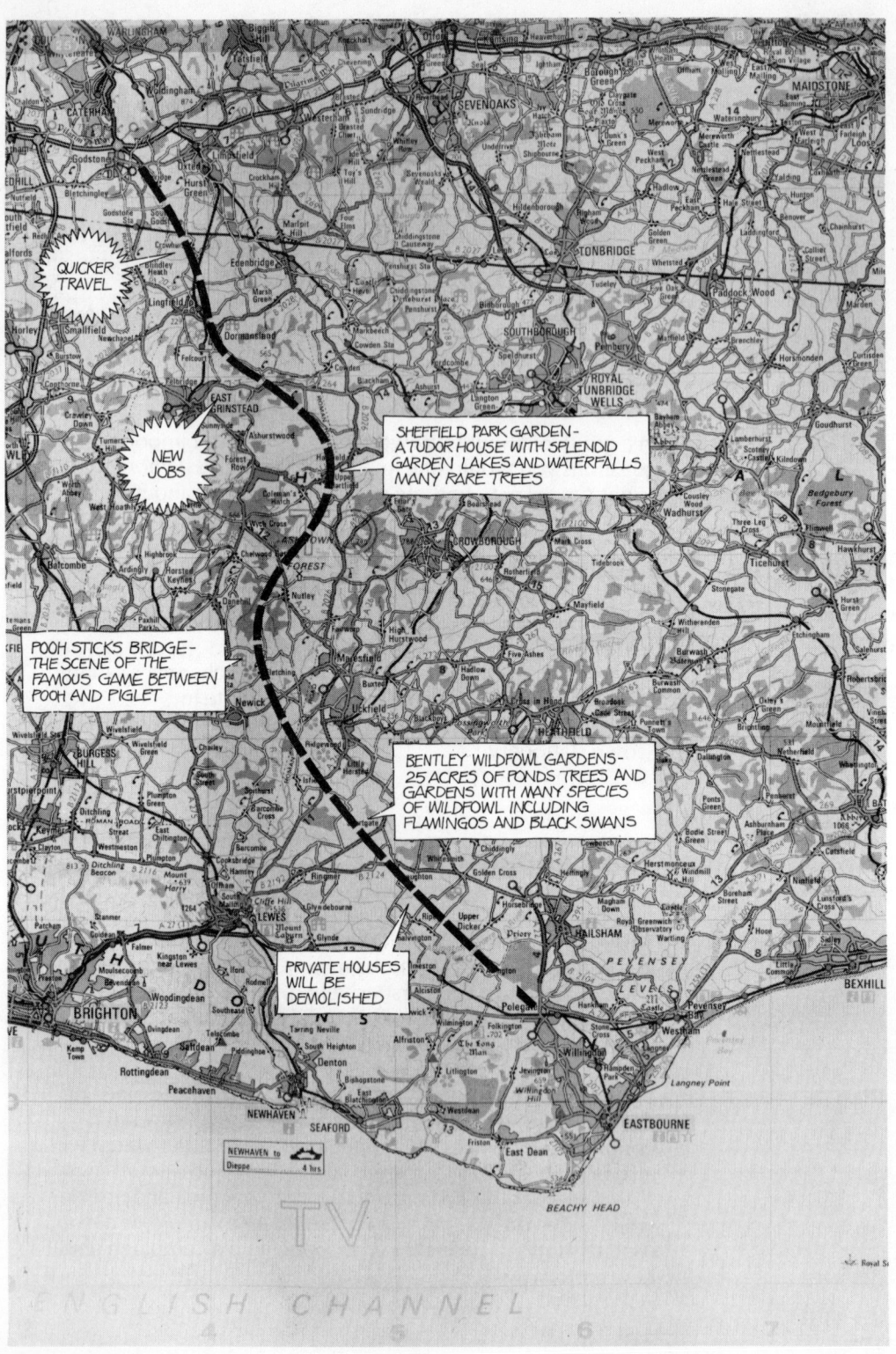

Map annotations:

QUICKER TRAVEL

NEW JOBS

SHEFFIELD PARK GARDEN – A TUDOR HOUSE WITH SPLENDID GARDEN LAKES AND WATERFALLS MANY RARE TREES

POOH STICKS BRIDGE – THE SCENE OF THE FAMOUS GAME BETWEEN POOH AND PIGLET

BENTLEY WILDFOWL GARDENS – 25 ACRES OF PONDS TREES AND GARDENS WITH MANY SPECIES OF WILDFOWL INCLUDING FLAMINGOS AND BLACK SWANS

PRIVATE HOUSES WILL BE DEMOLISHED

Work out all the arguments which might be made about your piece of development.

Write

Then prepare publicity material to persuade people to see it your way. You might try the following:
■ leaflets
■ posters
■ letters to the press, MPs, etc.
■ a speech for a public meeting
■ car stickers and badges
■ newspaper articles
■ local radio feature programme

You may find it useful to build up a 'fact file' and a map outlining the people and places affected by the development.

Imaginary planet

This activity asks you to exercise your imagination to create a strange and alien world. Try to bring your imaginary world alive in the mind of your reader by providing him or her with a selection of documents and mementoes collected during a visit. This gives you an opportunity for writing in a wide variety of styles and shapes.

Imagine

Imagine a planet.

Give it a name.

Draw a map of it.

Write

Make an imaginary visit to this world, keeping . . .
■ a log book of your activities, impressions and reactions
■ a catalogue of the amazing life-forms you encounter
■ a copy of the planetary laws
■ a brief history of the planet

- a guide to one of its settlements, cities, villages, homes or public buildings
- an interview with an interesting inhabitant
- an adventure which takes place during your visit
- a report of your arrival and visit in the local media (e.g. galactic daily newspaper, hyperspace tele-laser box or interplanetary computer news broadcasts, etc.)
- an article for readers back on Earth – 'A Day in the Life of an Inhabitant', or any other interesting ideas you may have

Poetry and prose

This activity should alert you to the many forms writing can take, each having different capacities and strengths for you to exploit. Here, you are asked to consider the different opportunities presented in poetry and prose.

Read

Here are an extract from D. H. Lawrence's novel *Sons and Lovers* and a poem written by him. They concern the same incident, said to be autobiographical.

from: Sons and Lovers

When William was growing up, the family moved from the Bottoms to a house on the brow of the hill, commanding a view of the valley, which spread out like a convex cockleshell, or a clamp-shell, before it. In front of the house was a huge old ash-tree. The west wind, sweeping from Derbyshire, caught the houses with full force, and the tree shrieked again. Morel liked it.

'It's music,' he said. 'It sends me to sleep.'

But Paul and Arthur and Annie hated it. To Paul it became almost a demoniacal noise. The winter of their first year in the new house their father was very bad. The children played in the street, on the brim of the wide, dark valley, until eight o'clock. Then they went to bed. Their mother sat sewing below. Having such a great space in front of the house gave the children a feeling of night, of vastness, and of terror. This terror came in from the shrieking of the tree and the anguish of the home discord. Often Paul would wake up, after he had been asleep a long time, aware of thuds downstairs. Instantly he was wide awake. Then he heard the booming shouts of his father, come home nearly drunk, then the sharp replies of his mother, then the bang, bang of his father's fist on the table, and the nasty snarling shout as the man's voice got higher. And then the whole was drowned in a piercing medley of shrieks and cries from the great, windswept ash-tree. The children lay silent in suspense, waiting for a lull in the wind to hear what their father was doing. He might hit their mother again. There was a feeling of horror, a kind of bristling in the darkness, and a sense of blood. They lay with their hearts in the grip of an intense anguish. The wind came through the tree fiercer and fiercer. All the cords of the great harp hummed, whistled, and shrieked. And then came the horror of the sudden silence, silence everywhere, outside and downstairs. What was it? Was it a silence of blood? What had he done?

The children lay and breathed the darkness. And then, at last, they heard their father throw down his boots and tramp upstairs in his stockinged feet. Still they listened. Then at last, if the wind allowed, they heard the water of the tap drumming into the kettle, which their mother was filling for morning, and they could go to sleep in peace.

D. H. LAWRENCE

Discord in Childhood

Outside the house an ash-tree hung its terrible whips,
And at night when the wind rose, the lash of the tree
Shrieked and slashed the wind, as a ship's
Weird rigging in a storm shrieks hideously.

Within the house two voices arose, a slender lash
Whistling she-delirious rage, and the dreadful sound
Of a male thong booming and bruising, until it had drowned
The other voice in a silence of blood, 'neath the noise of the ash.

D. H. LAWRENCE

Discuss

In a group, discuss these extracts and consider how poetry and prose differ. This is a very difficult question, to which there are many answers. You might return to the question after trying to write each way yourself.

Write

Imagine an incident or an object. Present it in poetry and prose. We suggest that, like Lawrence, you start with a brief, intense personal experience. Notice, as you write, the strengths and limitations of each form.

5 Making stories

The poet Ted Hughes has called stories 'little factories of understanding'. It is through the telling of stories, through the reading of stories and through listening to stories that we can make sense of experience and the world around us.

Each of the activities in this section aims to get you writing your own stories in a variety of shapes and styles. Storytelling itself is an ancient art and stories come in many forms. The letter sequence is an idea borrowed from the early novelists of the eighteenth century who told their stories through exchanges of letters, whereas DIY stories are as recent as the computer.

An illustrated children's story

Young children are eager for stories, and writing for them is especially rewarding and very demanding. This is what you are asked to do here. Make sure you have a clear idea of how old your audience is and what their interests are and notice how this influences the language you choose, and the sort of story you tell.

Read
The next few pages show some extracts from popular picture-story books for young children. They are taken from:

Not Now Bernard by David McKee
Albert and the Green Bottle by Elizabeth and Gerald Rose
Gorilla by Anthony Browne
Dinner at Alberta's by Russell Hoban
Angry Arthur by Hiawyn Oram and Satoshi Kitamura

Reflect
Discuss how these writers have taken account of the needs of their young audience, and use your findings to guide your own writing.

Write
Try writing and illustrating a story of your own. Try it out at a local primary school or with a younger brother or sister.

"There's a monster in the garden and it's going to eat me," said Bernard.

The night before her birthday, Hannah went to bed tingling
with excitement – she had asked her father for a gorilla!

In the middle of the night, Hannah woke up and saw a very
small parcel at the foot of the bed. It *was* a gorilla, but
it was just a toy.

Albert lived with his mother and father in a small cottage by the sea. He watched the big ships pass and wondered where they had been. He thought how exciting it must be to sail on the deep dark sea.

He read in the newspapers of a man who was sailing round the world, and envied him.

How he wished that he could buy a boat, but they were far too expensive, so he decided to build his own.

"Arthur," said Mrs. Crocodile to her son one evening at dinner, "you are eating like a regular little beast."

"He won't close his mouth when he chews," said Arthur's sister, Emma, "and I have to sit opposite him, so I have a good view of everything."

"Whuzzhuh maher?" said Arthur.

"Don't talk when your mouth is full," said Father. "Little bits of ravioli are landing on your sister and no one can understand what you are saying."

"It's awful," said Emma.

"It certainly is," said Mother.

"Everybody always picks on me," said Arthur when his mouth was empty.

"No," said his mother,
"it's too late. Go to bed."
"I'll get angry," said Arthur.
"Get angry,"
said his mother.

Once there was a boy called Arthur.
He wanted to stay up and watch
the western on T.V.

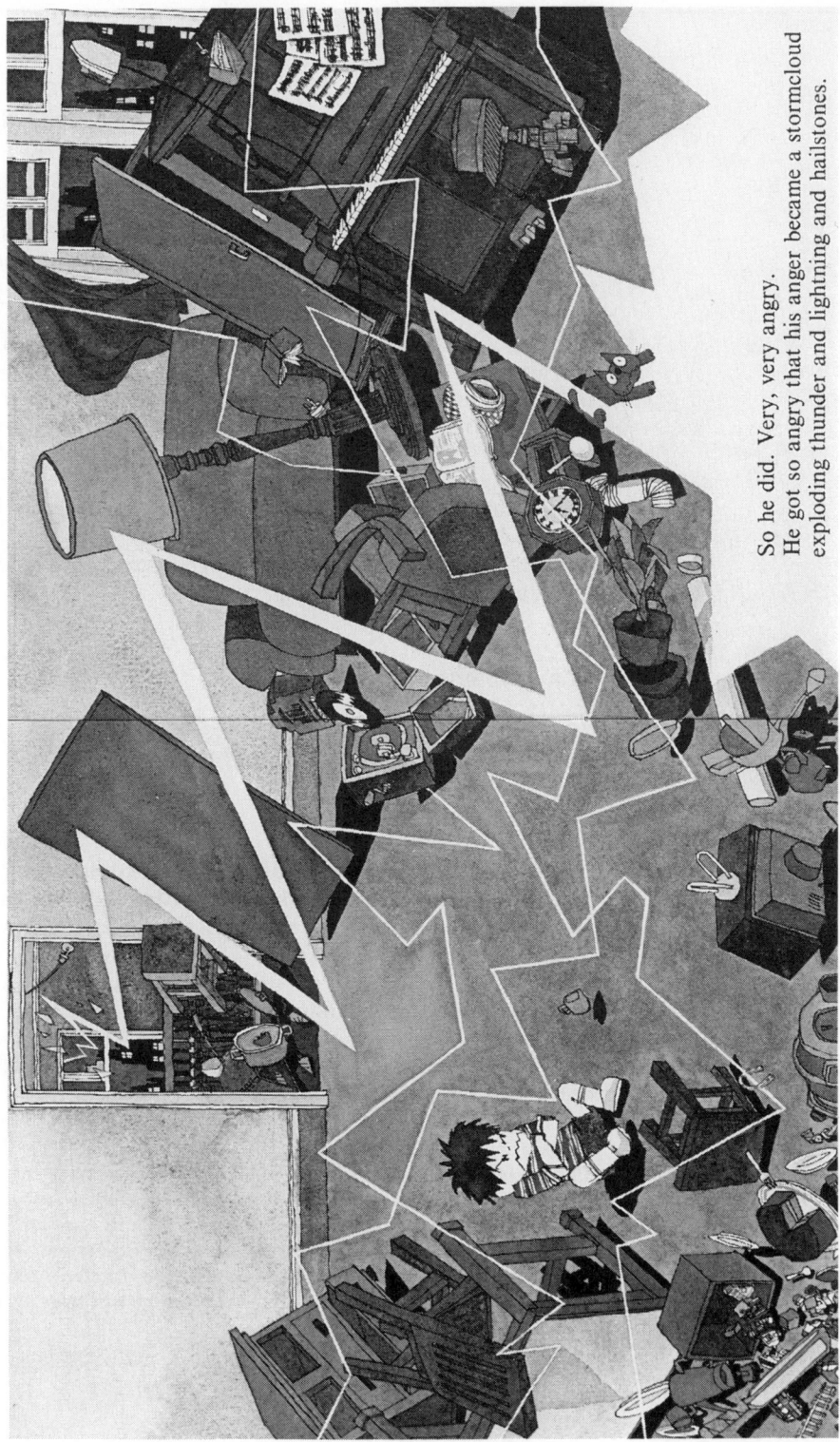

So he did. Very, very angry.
He got so angry that his anger became a stormcloud exploding thunder and lightning and hailstones.

Modern myths

This is an exercise in storytelling, which is one of the oldest forms of literature. Modern myths are present-day horror stories which are passed on by word of mouth, and though frightening, people often believe them, even though there is no evidence of their truth. We all use stories to express and control our fears. As you write, notice how storytelling is an art, in which the teller tempts the listeners along, holding them in suspense until the end.

You probably know lots of modern myths. Have you heard the one about:

- the woman who dried her poodle in the microwave oven?
- the cheap car that had an unpleasant smell which would not go away?
- the elderly hitch-hiker with the hairy hand?
- the man in the cinema whose chicken take-away included some strange bones?
- the restaurant that was closed down because of something nasty in the fridge?
- the cat that ate the small puppy?

Read

Here are some examples:

from: The Book of Nasty Legends

Overexposure

As they left the caravan site just after dawn that morning the wife stayed in bed in the trailer while her husband drove. As she drowsily awoke she felt the motion of the trailer stop and, thinking they had reached their destination, a remote and secluded site in the hills, she stepped out of the caravan in her sleeping attire – her birthday suit.

At that precise moment, the trailer sped away and there she was left, stark naked, at a set of traffic lights in the middle of town during the morning rush-hour.

Notes
This very popular legend has been widely recorded since the 1960s on both sides of the Atlantic. It has even been reported as 'a true story' in the *Weekend Camper* (1973). The simplicity and humour of the tale has meant that it has been incorporated into many other mediated forms of entertainment. For example, it was used as the climactic incident in the Doris Day film *With Six You Get Egg Roll*. Similarly, it was incorporated into *The Likely Lads* film.

Dangers of the microwave oven

I once heard of an elderly lady who used to breed pedigree cats and exhibit them at shows. She specialised in Persian cats and their long hair always made it a difficult task to clean and groom them for showing. In order to cut down the effort involved the old lady had evolved the practice of first washing the cat, towelling it dry and then, finally, giving it a very brief warming in her electric oven.

One Christmas her cooker developed a fault and so her son, by way of a Christmas present, bought her a brand new microwave oven. On the day of the next cat show, not understanding the basic difference in the technology between an ordinary electric cooker and a microwave oven, the old lady industriously washed her prize-winning Persian cat and popped it into the oven for a few seconds. There really was no miaow, nor any noise at all from the cat, for the poor creature exploded the instant the oven was switched on.

Notes

Told about cats, dogs and babies, this sad story has regularly appeared in North America and Europe over the past few years. Pre-microwave technology versions of the legend have the individual drying the unwitting victim in a regular oven or wood stove. In Russia the tale is related of a mother bathing her baby in a tub of warm water. Placing the tub on top of the apparently unlit stove, the mother goes out and stands gossiping with a neighbour for some time. On returning indoors she is horrified to discover the draught of the open door has rekindled the fire and cooked the baby in the tub.

The hairy-handed hitch-hiker

Driving home alone one evening a young woman notices an old lady with a large shopping bag trying to hitch a lift in her direction. Feeling charitable, and in spite of her vow never to pick up hitch-hikers when alone, the girl stops and offers the hitch-hiker a ride. With much gratitude the old lady accepts and gets into the car. The young woman is about to drive away when she notices that her 'female' passenger has large hairy hands and wrists.

Guessing instantly that the old lady is in fact a man, she pretends to be having trouble with the car and asks 'him' to get out and check if the rear lights are working. As soon as the 'old lady' is round the back of the car the young woman immediately locks the doors and drives away.

In fear she goes straight to the police station where she is questioned and the car is searched. In the shopping bag the hairy-handed hitch-hiker has left behind, the police find a large and very sharp blood-stained axe – all ready for the next victim.

Notes

Versions of this comparatively well-known story have been circulating in

England certainly since the early 1800s. The *Stamford Mercury* for 11 April 1834 reports a similar tale and Elizabeth Perkins in her book, *A Tree in the Valley*, relates how, around 1850, George Marsden of Hollowmeadows near Sheffield allegedly experienced a similar incident. In this case George attributed it to highway robbers.

The legend often functions as a warning and so, although it may lie dormant in people's memories, at times of social tension it can reappear. This story was frequently told as true and used as a warning against picking up hitch-hikers during the period Sutcliffe, the 'Yorkshire Ripper', was active in the Leeds area.

The vanishing grandmother

During a camping holiday in Spain grandmother, who had been brought along with the rest of the family, died during the night of natural causes. Not wanting to bury her in a foreign country, where they might never be able to visit her grave again, the family decide to head for home and attempt to smuggle her through Spain and France and so back to England. With this in mind, they rolled grandmother's body in a carpet, tied it on to the roof rack of the car, along with the camping equipment, and started on their journey.

They drove all night and, just before breakfast, they heaved a sigh of relief as they crossed the border out of Spain and into France.

By this time all the family were very tired and hungry. As a stop for breakfast sounded a good idea, they parked the car in a side street next to a suitable café. Not wanting to leave the corpse for too long and also wishing to continue their journey as soon as possible, they ate a hasty breakfast and returned to the car. However, to their horror, their possessions had been stolen from the roof of the car including the carpet and grandmother's corpse. The funny thing is the body never did turn up.

Notes
Although a somewhat gruesome and unfortunate story, the legend has had widespread popularity throughout Europe and North America since the Second World War. More often than not set in Europe, the legend has frequently been incorporated into films and literature. For instance, Alfred Hitchcock used the theme in *The Diplomatic Corpse* and it is related over dinner to Georges de Sarre in Roger Peyrefitte's novel *La Fin des ambassades* (1953).

PAUL SMITH

Talk

Start off in a group, sharing stories you know.
· Notice the techniques used by a good storyteller to grab attention, and keep the listener interested.
Discuss what the stories have in common.
Talk through the reasons why so many of these stories get repeated.

Write Collect your favourite stories together in the form of a small book. Write a preface to your collection, introducing your reader to the idea of modern myths.

Do-it-yourself stories

This activity will make you more aware of the planning that goes into a story. It will suggest problems and techniques which writers use in composing stories. Notice how the story draws the reader in by picturing events and making choices.

from: Citadel of Chaos

The sun sets. As twilight turns to darkness you start your climb up the hill towards that forbidding shape silhouetted against the night sky. The Citadel is less than an hour's climb.

Some distance from its walls you stop to rest – a mistake, as it seems a fearful spectre from which there is no escape. The hairs on your neck prickle as you look towards it.

But you are ashamed of your fears. With grim resolve you march onwards towards the main gate, where you know guards will be waiting. You consider your options. You have already thought about claiming to be a herbalist, come to treat a guard with a fever. You could pose as a trader or an artisan – perhaps a carpenter. You could even be a nomad, seeking shelter for the night.

As you ponder the possibilities, and the yarns you will have to spin to the guards, you reach the main trail leading up to the gates. Two lanterns burn on either side of the portcullis.

You hear muffled gruntings as you approach, and two mis-shapen creatures step forward. On the left stands an ugly creature with the head of a dog and the body of a great ape, flexing its powerful arms. Its opposite number is indeed its opposite, with the head of an ape on the body of a large dog. This latter guard approaches you on all fours. It stops some metres in front of you, raises itself on its hind legs and addresses you.

Which story will you opt for?

Will you pose as a herbalist?	Turn to **261**
Will you claim to be a tradesman?	Turn to **230**
Will you ask for shelter for the night?	Turn to **20**

20 The Ape-Dog tells you that no one is allowed into the Black Tower after dark – you will have to look elsewhere for shelter. You may either resign yourself to a fight (turn to **288**). Or you may pick up a stone and cast a Fool's Gold Spell on it, offering them a nugget of gold as a bribe to let you in (turn to **96**). Deduct the Fool's Gold Spell from your Spells if you use it.

230 'Come to make some money, eh?' says the Ape-Dog. 'Well you can share some of your profits with us!' As you have nothing to offer them, you can pull a rock out of your pouch and cast a Fool's Gold Spell on it, offering them a gold nugget (turn to **96**), or you can prepare yourself for battle (turn to **288**). Deduct the Fool's Gold Spell from your Spells if you use it.

261 The Ape-Dog asks to see your herbs. Luckily, you grabbed a few handfuls of weeds on your way and you show them. Cocking its head to one side, the creature eyes you suspiciously. It asks you for the name of the guard you have come to treat – something you hadn't planned on! You quickly think of a name to bluff the creature with:

Kylltrog	Turn to **81**
Pincus	Turn to **175**
Blag	Turn to **394**

S. JACKSON

If you are a computer fan, or if you have read any adventure books of the dungeons-and-dragons type, you will be familiar with stories such as these.

As the reader you are asked to imagine yourself as the main character in an adventure. As the reader progresses, you make choices about what happens next and follow your own path through the adventure.

Here is part of a plan for such a story:

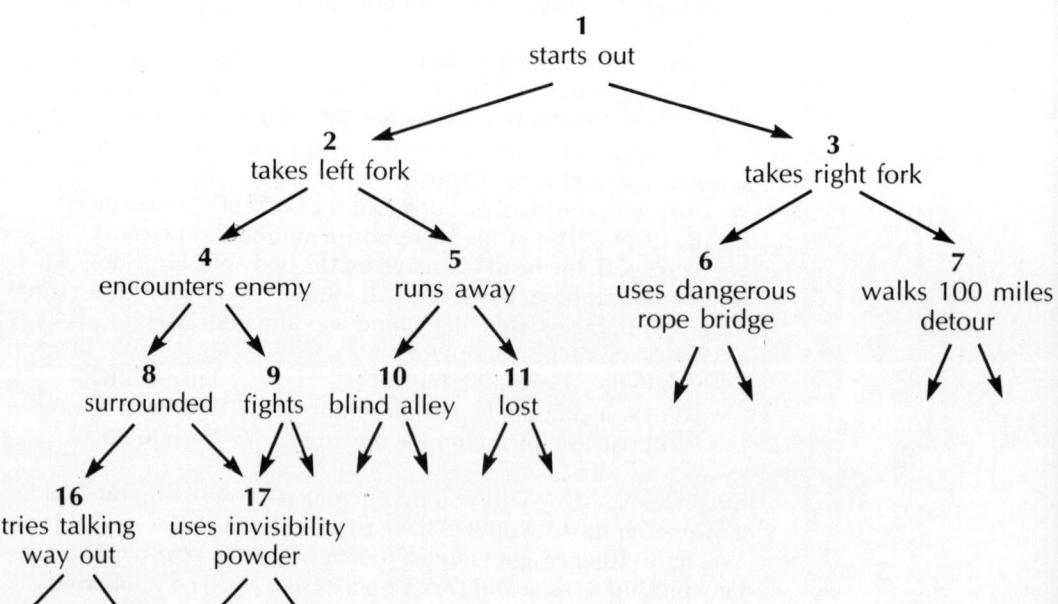

Write

■ Now plan and write your own DIY story.
■ Some people like to write their adventure into a small exercise book, with a choice posed on each page, and with illustrations. You can also load your story as a computer program (like that on the Macmillan *Branching Story* disc).

The citadel

This activity asks you to use your powers of imagination and storytelling to write an adventure story. It involves creating characters and telling the story of their struggle to reach a goal. You might like to write this with a special audience or reader in mind – perhaps a younger sister or brother, or a local primary-school class. Knowing your audience helps in choosing your material and your style.

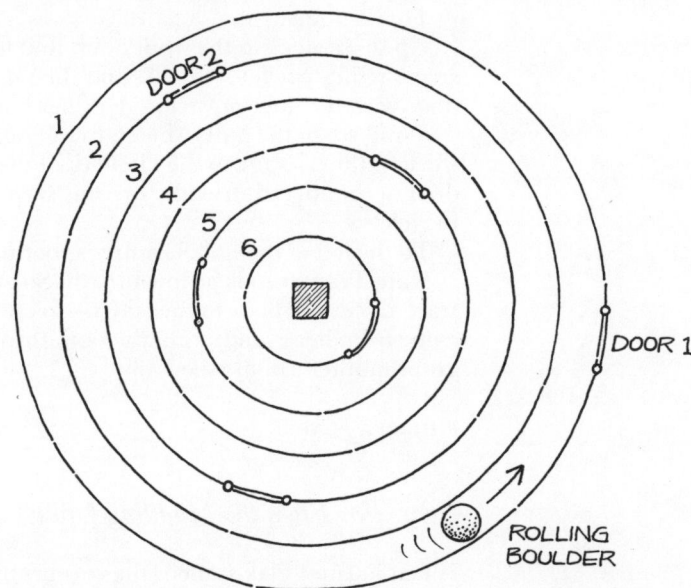

Write

The citadel is a huge circular fortress, with six great walls, one within another. Each wall has only one door leading inwards. Inside each wall is a terror protecting the centre against intruders. No one has got beyond the third wall before now.

You know that the first ring is protected by a huge rolling boulder, which travels the ring every 30 seconds. The door in the next wall is several hundred yards away.

At the centre of the citadel is something you must have. You and your three companions have come to get it. This is a world of magic powers and strange forces of dark and light.

Tell the story of your adventures in the citadel.

Story openings

This activity asks you to look carefully at the way writers select material for the opening of a story, and how they try to catch the reader's imagination and interest. It is an exercise in drawing in and preparing your reader.

Read

Read these openings:

from: *The Way to Sattin Shore*

Here is Kate Tranter coming home from school in the January dusk – the first to come, because she is the youngest of her family. Past the churchyard. Past the shops. Along the fronts of the tall, narrow terrace houses she goes. Not this one, nor this one, nor this . . .

Stop at the house with no lit window.

This is home.

Up three steps to the front door, and feel for the key on the string in her pocket. Unlock, and then in. Stand just inside the door with the door now closed, at her back.

Stand so, in the hall. Ahead, to the right, the stairs. Ahead, to the left, the passage to the kitchen: in the wider part, by the back door, a round, red, friendly eye has seen her – the reflector of her bicycle.

To the left of the hall, Granny's room.

Kate Tranter took a slow breath. She made herself ready to start across the floor to the stairs – to cross the dark beam that came from her grandmother's room through the gap where her grandmother's door stood ajar.

PHILIPPA PEARCE

from: *Far From the Madding Crowd*

When Farmer Oak smiled, the corners of his mouth spread till they were within an unimportant distance of his ears, his eyes were reduced to chinks, and diverging wrinkles appeared round them, extending upon his countenance like the rays in a rudimentary sketch of the rising sun.

THOMAS HARDY

from: *Dinky Hocker Shoots Smack!*

'Don't tell people we've moved to Brooklyn,' Tucker Woolf's father always told him. 'Tell them we've moved to Brooklyn *Heights*.'

'Why? Brooklyn Heights is Brooklyn.'

'Believe me, Tucker, you'll make a better impression.'

Which was very important to Tucker's father – making a good impression. That fact was one of the reasons Tucker felt sorry for his father now. It was hard to make a good impression when you'd just been fired.

M. E. KERR

from: *The Little Sister*

The pebbled glass door panel is lettered in flaked black paint: '*Philip Marlowe .... Investigations*'. It is a reasonably shabby door at the end of a reasonably shabby corridor in the sort of building that was new about the year the all-tile bathroom became the basis of civilization. The door is locked, but next to it is another door with the same legend which is not locked. Come on in – there's nobody in here but me and a big bluebottle fly. But not if you're from Manhattan, Kansas.

RAYMOND CHANDLER

from: *Typee*

Six months at sea! Yes, reader, as I live, six months out of sight of land; cruising after the sperm-whale beneath the scorching sun of the Line, and tossed on the billows of the wide-rolling Pacific – the sky above, the sea around, and nothing else! Weeks and weeks ago our fresh provisions were all exhausted. There is not a sweet potatoe left; not a single yam. Those glorious bunches of bananas which once decorated our stern and quarter-deck, have, alas, disappeared! and the delicious oranges which hung suspended from our tops and stays – they, too, are gone! Yes, they are all departed, and there is nothing left us but salt-horse and sea-biscuit. Oh! ye state-room sailors, who make so much ado about a fourteen-days' passage across the Atlantic; who so pathetically relate the privations and hardships of the sea, where, after a day of breakfasting, lunching, dining off five courses, chatting, playing whist, and drinking champagne-punch, it was your hard lot to be shut up in little cabinets of mahogany and maple, and sleep for ten hours, with nothing to disturb you but 'those good-for-nothing tars, shouting and tramping overhead', – what would ye say to our six months out of sight of land?

Oh! for a refreshing glimpse of one blade of grass – for a snuff at the fragrance of a handful of the loamy earth! Is there nothing fresh around us? Is there no green thing to be seen?

HERMAN MELVILLE

from: The Haunting

When, suddenly, on an ordinary Wednesday, it seemed to Barney
that the world tilted and ran downhill in all directions, he knew
he was about to be haunted again. It had happened when he was
younger but he had thought that being haunted was a babyish
thing that you grew out of, like crying when you fell over, or not
having a bike.

'Remember Barney's imaginary friends, Mantis, Bigbuzz and
Ghost?' Claire – his stepmother – sometimes said. 'The garden
seems empty now that they've gone. I quite miss them.'

But she was really pleased perhaps because, being so very real
to Barney, they had become too real for her to laugh over. Barney
had been sorry to lose them, but he wanted Claire to feel
comfortable living with him. He could not remember his own
mother and Claire had come as a wonderful surprise, giving him
a hug when he came home from school, asking him about his day,
telling him about hers, arranging picnics and unexpected parties
and helping him with hard homework. It seemed worth losing
Mantis, Bigbuzz and Ghost and the other kind phantoms that
had been his friends for so many days before Claire came.

MARGARET MAHY

from: Pride and Prejudice

It is a truth universally acknowledged, that a single man in
possession of a good fortune, must be in want of a wife.

JANE AUSTEN

from: Brighton Rock

Hale knew they meant to murder him before he had been in
Brighton three hours.

GRAHAM GREENE

Reflect   In a group, discuss which of these you found most interesting
and why. Consider the tasks that face a writer opening a story,
and then discuss how each of the writers here tackled them.

Write   Now write your own openings, trying all the time to tempt your
reader in.

Letter sequence

A letter sequence is a set of letters that are linked in a particular way, to tell a story. The reader of the sequence does most of the work, reading between the lines of the letters, and working out the events and personalities which lie behind them. Writing a sequence will give you practice in writing letters to a variety of people, each with its different tone and style of language.

Read

Here are some extracts from a letter sequence written by a fourth-year student:

MINISTRY OF DEFENCE

St.James Street,
LONDON, W.1.

Mr. Max Davidson,
10, Acacia Avenue,
Radlett,
Herts.,

    Under the power conveyed to me by the Defence of the Realm Act 1932, I instruct you to report to Royal Air Force Station, Biggin Hill, Kent at the earliest possible moment. A travel warrant is enclosed for your use.

    You will only need sufficient clothing and money to last you for a few days.

Air Commodore, J.Hartley,
September 28th, 1940   Secretary to the Ministry of Defence.

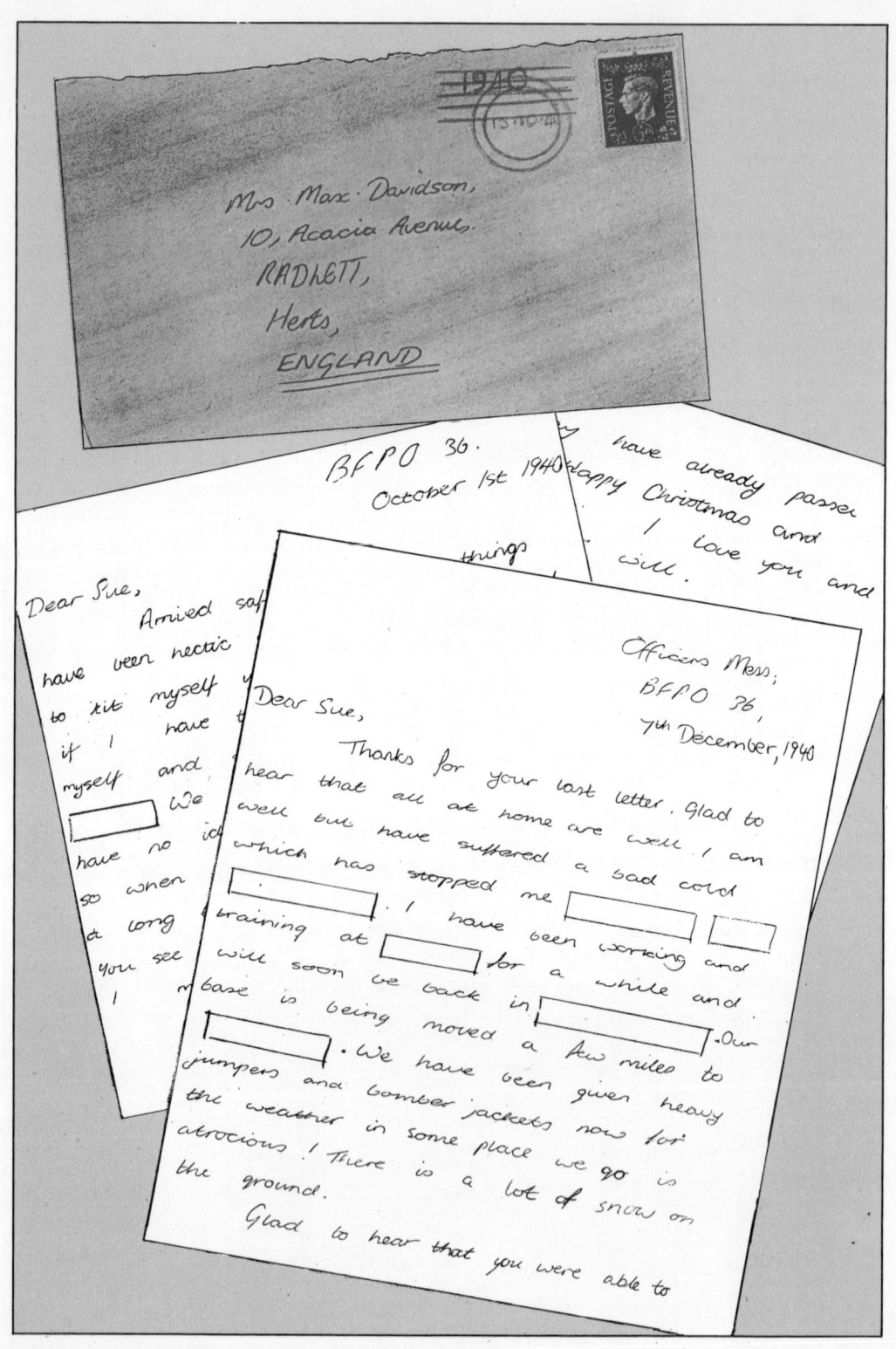

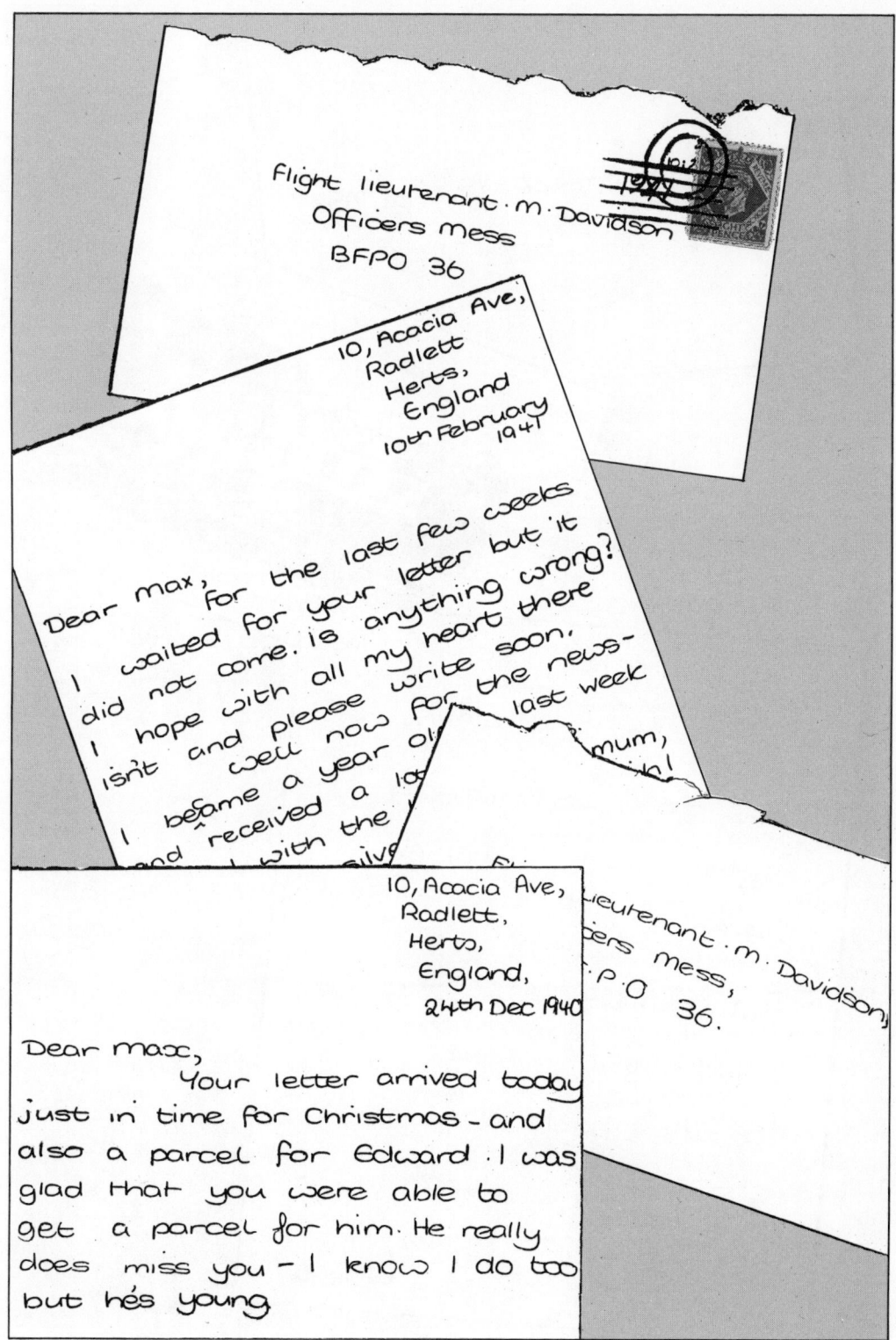

Flight lieutenant · M · Davidson
Officers mess
BFPO 36

10, Acacia Ave,
Radlett
Herts,
England
10th February
1941

Dear max,
for the last few weeks
I waited for your letter but it
did not come. is anything wrong?
I hope with all my heart there
isn't and please write soon,
well now for the news-
last week
I became a year ol~ mum,
and received a lo~
~ with the ~

10, Acacia Ave,
Radlett,
Herts,
England,
24th Dec 1940

lieutenant · m · Davidson,
~ers mess,
~ P·O 36.

Dear max,
Your letter arrived today
just in time for Christmas - and
also a parcel for Edward. I was
glad that you were able to
get a parcel for him. He really
does miss you - I know I do too
but he's young

To

Father christmas

The home for Forty Years of Charles Darwin

Dear Father christmas
Please could I
have for christmas a
football, a Jigsaw
Puzzle and some Paints.

But most of all
could you send me my
Daddy back.

love Edward x x x

(age 6)

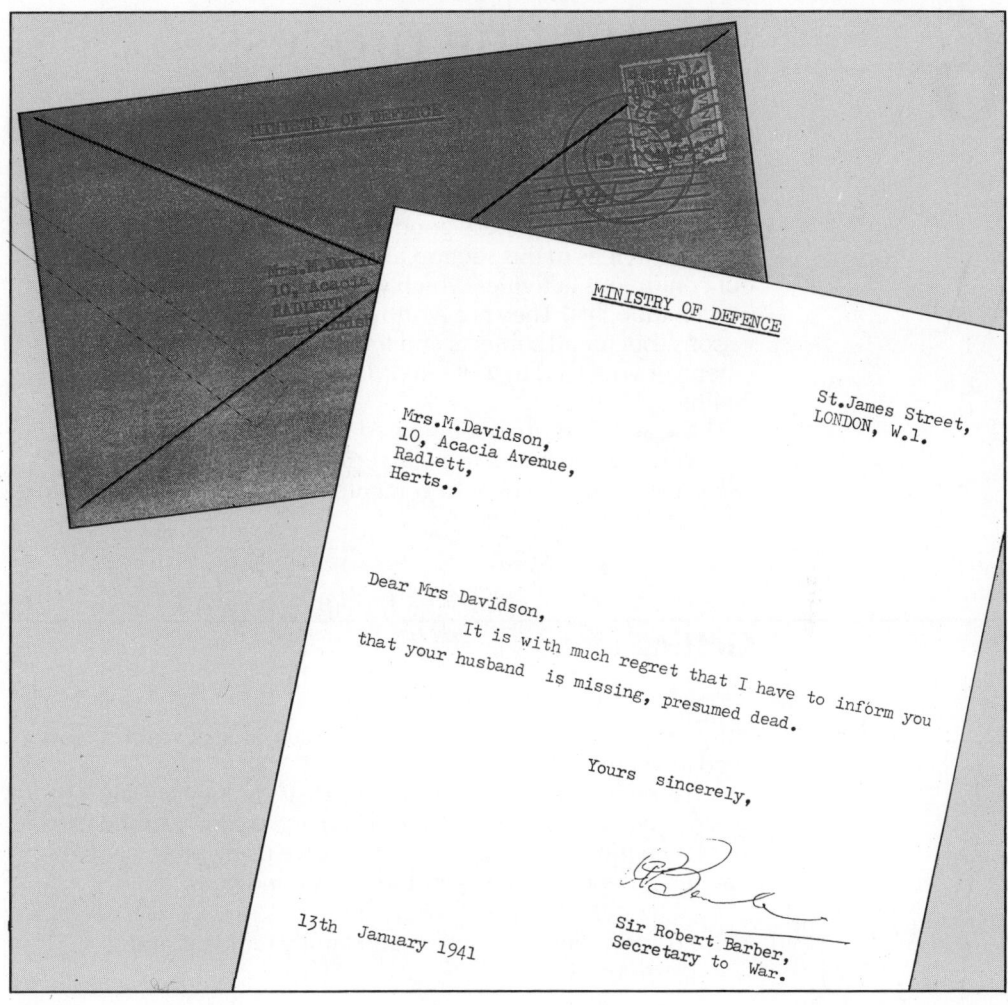

MINISTRY OF DEFENCE

St.James Street,
LONDON, W.1.

Mrs.M.Davidson,
10, Acacia Avenue,
Radlett,
Herts.,

Dear Mrs Davidson,
    It is with much regret that I have to inform you
that your husband is missing, presumed dead.

Yours sincerely,

13th January 1941

Sir Robert Barber,
Secretary to War.

Write

Try writing your own sequence. Here are some ideas:
- You are left some money in a will. Book a luxury holiday which goes wrong.
- Letters that tell a story of intrigue, suspicion or crime (e.g. kidnapping).
- Letters between members of a family when an unexpected event brings them back in contact.

Remember to include as wide a variety of styles of letter as possible. Use your own stationery, postcards, notelets, etc.

Further reading

If you have enjoyed this activity, your teacher might recommend novels that are written in the form of letters. There is an amusing short story called *Computers Don't Argue* by Gordon Dickson, and *A Man of Letters* by Stacy Aumonier. Also *Dear Comrade* by Frances Thomas (Bodley Head) and *Dear Mr Henshaw* by Beverly Cleary (Macmillan, M Book series).

6 The writing process

In this final section we introduce a number of everyday writing activities, some of which you may have found yourself practising and improving in the course of using the book. We hope you will continue to develop these good writing habits.

The activities in this section are therefore not one-off exercises but continuous activities which will promote the quality of your written thoughts. They are worthwhile, not just in English lessons, but for all subjects and for your life outside school, wherever you need to write in order to express a meaning or a feeling.

These activities are not intended solely for silent individual use. Most people find it useful to collaborate over written work, using other people to generate ideas, co-operate in writing or to read through drafts.

Getting ideas

For your coursework, or any open-ended piece of writing, you need to get the initial idea right.

Some people have trouble getting ideas, or they get stuck or bored at a later stage. Here is some advice we have found useful in this situation. Most suggestions involve using other people – teachers, friends, family – for their ideas and help.

■ Brainstorm friends, teachers and family for ideas and suggestions.

■ Collect a huge list of ideas and phrases which pop into your head before you start.

> FIRST DAY AT SCHOOL
> Miss Cartwright - bun, high heels, rosy cheeks
> "Gels! Don't dare!"
> The play corner - plasticine
> Jenny spilling the ink
>   - black spattered
>   on white
> Assembly - Mr Grimthorpe.
> Golden catkins by the window. Hot sunny
> days. Bees. Traffic.
> Tin boxes, raffia, friezes, painting, stories.
> Milk.
> Martha Pogson's poem.

■ Map out your subject in the form of a diagram such as a star chart, flow diagram, 'for-and-against' columns, or simply grouping similar ideas together. (A friend or teacher can see at a glance what you have in mind and can easily suggest additional ideas.)

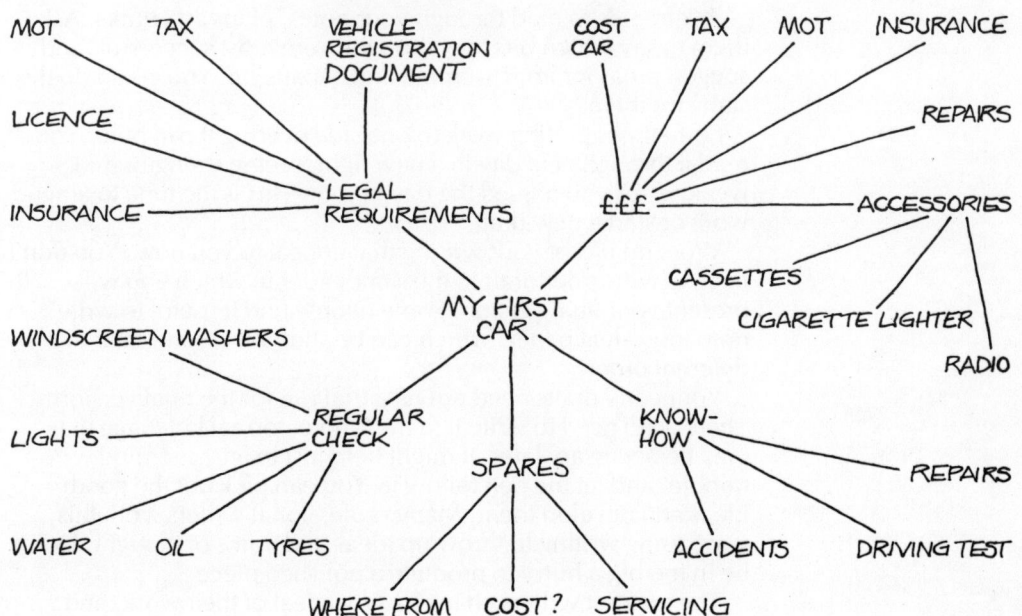

■ Set yourself a time limit (e.g. 5 minutes) and start writing. On no account must you stop until the time is up. Just keep it going, even if it seems unpromising. Most people find that a little of what they write is useful, and they use this little bit as the starting point for more ideas.

> *I don't know when I first started thinking about becoming a vet. I suppose it dates back to that time when Frank found the wounded moorhen with the broken wing. We brought it to the house but my...*

Drafting

Whether you are writing creatively or for a functional purpose, it is not easy to get your writing 'right' first time. It is better to experiment first, then write drafts to be discussed, changed and checked before the final version.

Ask friends to read through your notes, plans and drafts. Ask them to say which bits they thought were most successful, and suggest areas for improvement and expansion. You could do the same for them.

Sometimes putting work to one side overnight can help. You read it through next day in a new light, seeing strengths and weaknesses you missed the day before. This is the time to amend work or start a new draft.

Work on bits of your writing that appeal to you *now*. You don't have to write your draft in the same order in which you will present your final version. Some people find it useful to write onto loose-leaf papers which can be shuffled around later into a different order.

Your early drafts need not be a trial run for the final version. There is no need to write it in the kind of formal language that may be necessary later. It might help just to let your mind ramble, and let the pen follow it. You can pick out the good ideas and develop them. Many professional writers work this way, using writing to throw up ideas and trains of thought. Don't be in too big a hurry to produce a polished piece.

The greatest writers change a great deal of their work, and

rewrite huge sections of it. Their work is crossed with arrows, additions, deletions and other alterations. Here are the manuscripts of some famous writers. You can see them in the British Museum:

From *Pickwick Papers*, by Charles Dickens

Chap. 10.   July 8

With all this knowledge of Mr E — & with this authority to impatience it — more [quickly] could Lady Gate Build &c — her mind deeply busy in revolving what she had heard, feeling, thinking, recalling & foreseeing everything; shocked at — Miss Elliot, sighing over future. They adjourned, waited for Lady Russell. —

... Lady Dalrymple, confident — had been entire. — And the Embarrassment which must be felt from their ... in ones presence! — How to be brave to him — how to get rid of him — what to do by any of the Party at home — where to be believed & where to be active? — It was altogether as confusion of Images & Doubts — a perplexity, an agitation which she could not see the end of, —

And she was in Gay St — & still so far engrossed, that she started on being addressed by Admiral Croft, as if a person unlikely to be met there.

From Persuasion, by Jane Austen

84

#3
82.

I cou'd not this, this cruel stroke attend;
Fate claim'd Achilles, but might spare his friend:
I hop'd Patroclus might survive, to rear
The ~~his~~ tender ~~youth~~ Orphan with a parent care,
From Scyros Isle ~~re~~ conduct him oer ye main
~~And glad his eyes with~~ Pelthia his paternal reign
The ~~his~~ lofty Palace and ~~his~~ the large Domain.
For Peleus breathes no more the vital air;
Or ~~humbled~~ drags a wretched Life of ~~to ye dust~~ age & care,
~~Lives but~~ But still w news of my sad Fate invades
His hastening Soul ~~&~~ sinks him to ye Shades.

~~The~~ Sighing, he said: his grief ye Heroes join'd,
Each stole a ~~sigh~~ tear for wt he left behind.
Their mingled grief ye Sire of Heaven surveyd
And thus wth pity to his blue-eyd Maid.

Is ~~great~~ then Achilles now no more thy care,
& dost thou thus desert ye Great in War?
Lo where yon Sails their   arms extend
All comfortless he sits and wails his friend.
~~Haste, Ere~~ Thirst and want has ~~vigor Forces here~~
Haste & ~~pour infuse divine~~ ambrosia in his breast

He spoke, and sudden as the word of Jove
Shot ye descending Goddess from above
To ye ~~shrill Harpye~~ swift thro parted Æther ~~springs~~ the shrill Harpye
The wide air floating to her ample ^wings.
To great Achilles she her flight addrest
& pour'd divine ambrosia in his breast
with nectar sweet, (Refection of ye Gods!)
then swift ascending, sought ye bright ~~blest~~ abodes.

12
19

From Homer's *Iliad*, translated by Alexander Pope

A draft in progress: example 1

Look at this first draft of a professional writer preparing an article for a magazine, and then how she works on it to produce a more forceful piece of writing:

"Ask Why"
by Kristina

"I'm sorry, Sir," but we have ex-perienced equipment difficulties; ~~and our~~ *the* flight will be delayed ~~for~~ one hour," the flight attendant ex-plained to the business man in front of me.

"Oh," ~~replied~~ *shrugged* the man and ~~went~~ *strolled* to the waiting section ~~for flight 286 to Greenville, South Carolina.~~

I was next ~~in line and~~ didn't wait for another spiel.

"Why?" I asked curtly.

Five male ~~Heads from other~~ passengers turned like an E. F. Hutton com-mercial. ~~The face of one~~ *One face* said, "Pushy bitch," ~~four~~ *the* others~~:~~ said, "Good question . . . why?"

"Well, uh, I don't know." *she replied.*

~~Would you kindly find out for me,~~ "I ~~need~~ *have* to know," I ~~asked~~ *countered.*

The ~~flight~~ attendant motioned to a ~~gentleman dressed differently~~ *red-jacketed official.* ~~than the others in a red jacket.~~ *As they* ~~Then~~ whispered ~~to him probably the nature of my inquiry.~~ The man in charge glanced my way, smiled, and said, "Just one moment; I'll find out for you immediately."

"Ask Why"
by Kristina

"I'm sorry, Sir," the flight at-tendant explained to the business-man in front of me, "but we have experienced equipment difficulties; the flight will be delayed one hour."

"Oh," shrugged the man and strolled to the waiting section.

I didn't wait for another spiel. "Why?" I asked curtly.

Five male passengers turned like an E. F. Hutton commer-cial. One face said, "Pushy bitch;" the others: "Good question . . . why?"

"Well, uh, I don't know," she replied.

"*I have.* to know," I countered.

The attendant motioned to a red-jacketed official. As they whis-pered the man in charge glanced my way, smiled, and said, "Just one moment; I'll find out for you immediately."

The writer cuts out all the unnecessary information, and boosts the detail. She sharpens up some of the words ('went' becomes 'strolled'; 'replied' becomes 'shrugged'). Even though the amended passage is shorter, it is much more forceful and interesting.

A draft in progress: example 2

Draft 1 (from the *Dream Journey* exercise, page 9)

I see rolling green hills
Pastures
A few trees
A white road of fine white sand and a few pebbles
It is late afternoon
The path, about a yard wide
Winding over the hills
I can't see where it ends
It is high, and silent. I am alone.
The trees are picture-trees, they look like green brains

Amendments

I see rolling green hills
~~Pastures~~
and A few trees
A white road of fine white sand ~~and a few pebbles~~
It is late afternoon
~~The path, about a yard wide~~
Winding over the hills
I can't see where it ends
It is high, and silent. I am alone. ~~;~~ keep?
~~The trees are picture-trees, they look like~~ [green brains]
~~(And feel ⌄ I feel~~
~~I feel too a~~
~~I fear~~
All I can hear is ... ?)

Second draft

I see rolling green hills and a few trees,
Where a path of white sand
Winds into the distance.
A late summer sun is on its way down
And I am walking a path
So high and silent,
All I can hear
Is me.

The writer cut out the bits she did not like, or which sounded dull and out of place. She put the words in the best order. She cut out wasted and repeated words, then tried out new expressions as she joined it all up. The second draft is smoother and more intense.

All writers use drafts. Sometimes the writing goes well, but often there are important passages which take time to get right.

If you have access to a word-processor, you might like to experiment with drafting on it. Use the print-outs to amend each draft, then type in the corrections, until you feel it is right.

Final corrections

As you approach your final version, you will want to tidy up the spelling, punctuation and expression, and make sure your work is accurate in every way. You will want it to be neat, attractive, and easy for the reader.

This is a time when your teacher and your friends can be very helpful, pointing out things for improvement and correction. But don't leave all the work to them. Correct what you can, and if they will give you a general idea of the problems, try to improve by correcting them yourself.

For example, have a second go at the spellings they say are wrong, and then check in a dictionary. Don't just copy out their spellings – try to learn them for yourself. Or if they say that one of your sentences is clumsy or unclear – try rewriting it yourself. In this way you will learn to identify and deal with your problems instead of relying on other people.

Presentation

Before printing, writers hand-wrote their work and made final copies which were beautifully written and presented. Here, for example, is a page from Lewis Carroll's manuscript of *Alice in Wonderland*, and a fifteenth-century copy of Geoffrey Chaucer's *Canterbury Tales*:

33

are ferrets! Where can I have dropped them, I wonder?" Alice guessed in a moment that it was looking for the nosegay and the pair of white kid gloves, and she began hunting for them, but they were now nowhere to be seen — everything seemed to have changed since her swim in the pool, and her walk along the river-bank with its fringe of rushes and forget-me-nots, and the glass table and the little door had vanished.

Soon the rabbit noticed Alice, as she stood looking curiously about her, and at once said in a quick angry tone," why, Mary Ann! what are you doing out here? Go home this moment, and look on my dressing-table for my gloves and nosegay, and fetch them here, as quick as you can run, do you hear?" and Alice was so much frightened that she ran off at once, without

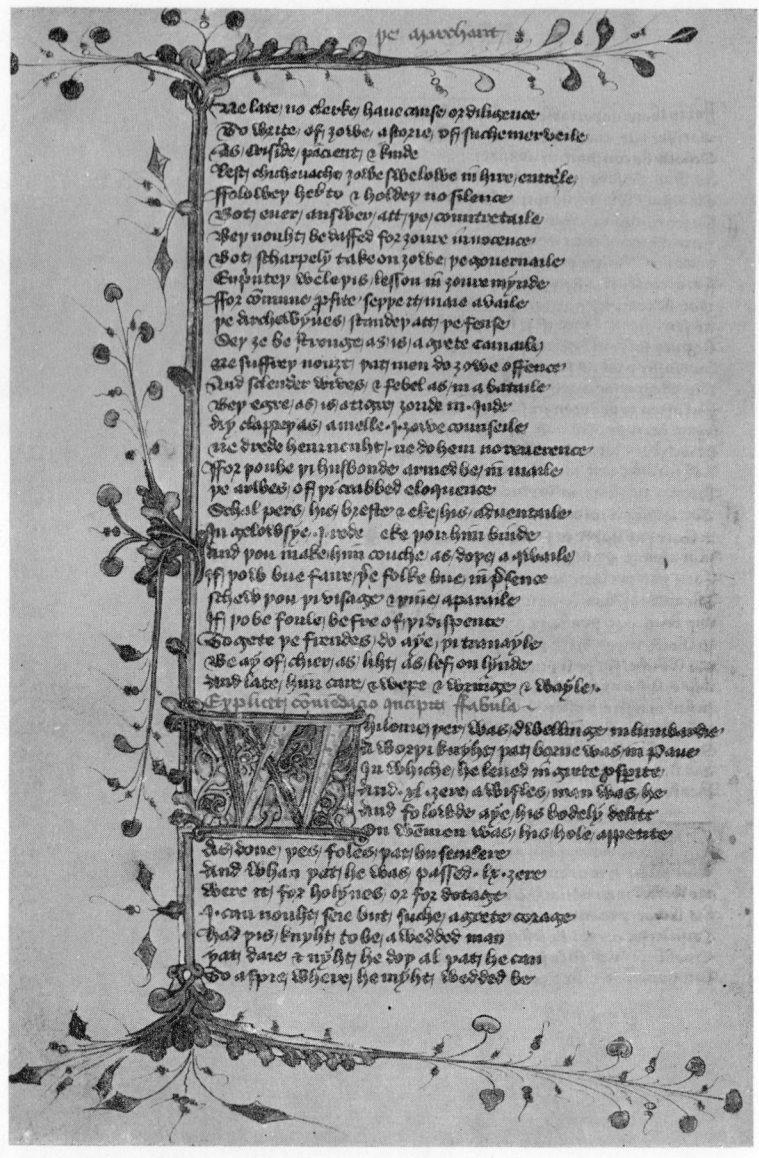

Look how neatly they are set out and how beautifully they are decorated and illustrated.

Taking a little more time, and a little more patience, nearly everyone can produce work like this which is well laid out, easy to read and pleasant to look at. Most of us like to see our own work looking good, and it is worth the effort. Here are some examples of work done by students from the exercises in this book:

Thursday June 30th 1870

The New York Herald

The Greatest Race On Record!

Thousands of people crammed the levee at New Orleans this afternoon ready for the start of the great steamboat race.

Over a million dollars has already been gambled and it is expected that thousands more will be staked right up to the end of the race.

The owner and captain of the Robert E. Lee, John Cannon, stripped his boat of everything which could be spared and took only 75 passengers aboard.

Thomas Leathers, captain of the Natchez took on his usual cargo and usual passenger number.

The time for the start of the race was 5.0 pm but the Lee cast off seven minutes early. Mr Leathers kept the Natchez stationary

until the last piece of freight was aboard and then went in persuit of the Lee. Brass bands played until both boats were out of sight.

INTERVIEW WITH J. CANNON

Q. Mr Cannon, what sort of precautions have you taken for the race?

A. Well, I took out everything we didn't need in the boat and only let on 75 passenges.

Q. Could you tell us about your boat?

A. Yes. It was built at Louisville and is 100 yards long. The boat has eight boilers and has large cylinders. The Lee is quite a big steamboat.

Q. Do you think that the Natchez has a better chance of winning being newer and longer than your boat?

A. Not really, because we have made up for

CAPTAIN OF THE LEE — JOHN CANNON

this by making our boat lighter so that it is only 4 ft in the water.

Q. What sort of time are you hoping to get?

A. Well, round about three days, 20 hours would be very pleasing.

Q. Are you confident that you will win the race?

A. It's difficult to say because any number of things could go wrong. And, of course, the Mississippi can be a turbulent and unpredictable river.

Report - Graham Allen.

Log entry number One —

Thursday June 30th.

We left New Orleans at 7 minutes to 5 o'clock this afternoon to the cheers of countless people on the levee.

The Natchez was kept at the wharf until the last piece of frieght was aboard and then came in persuit.

We past the timing point at St. Mary's Market at 3 minutes past 5 o'clock.

After 30 miles our 'doctor' broke down and we had to stop. Luckily, the pump was soon fixed and we carried on.

(10 o'clock p.m.)

Log entry number Two —

Friday 1st July.

We were still in the lead when we reached Baton Rouge at about 1-30 this morning. (Here the flat country gives way to thick forest).

We passed Natchez-on-the-hill in the late morning ahead of the Natchez — (this, of course, annoyed the townsfolk).

Here, we took coal on board from waiting barges.

We reached Vicksburg this evening a good distance ahead of the Natchez.

(9 o'clock p.m.)

Log entry number Three —

Sunday July 3rd.

In the early hours of this morning we had another misfortune — the steam drum began to leak. We stopped the engines and let the pressure down to 90 lbs. We managed to rivet the drum and carried on at a slower speed and at half pressure. We reached St. Louis and found that we had won! Our time for the journey was three days, 18 hours and 14 minutes.

Those Horns of the Mississippi are mine!

(11 o'clock p.m.)

CAPTAIN'S LOG

Captain John Cannon —

Bring in your own pens, stationery and paints to create something really special. Use card, coloured paper, illustrations, headings and borders – there are many ways of making work attractive and doing justice to interesting work. Your teacher will suggest times when you can do this.

Some of the activities in this book are quite long – collections of stories and clusters of exercises. They would look good in book-form, or as separate folders. Here are some ideas:

A simple booklet

A folder

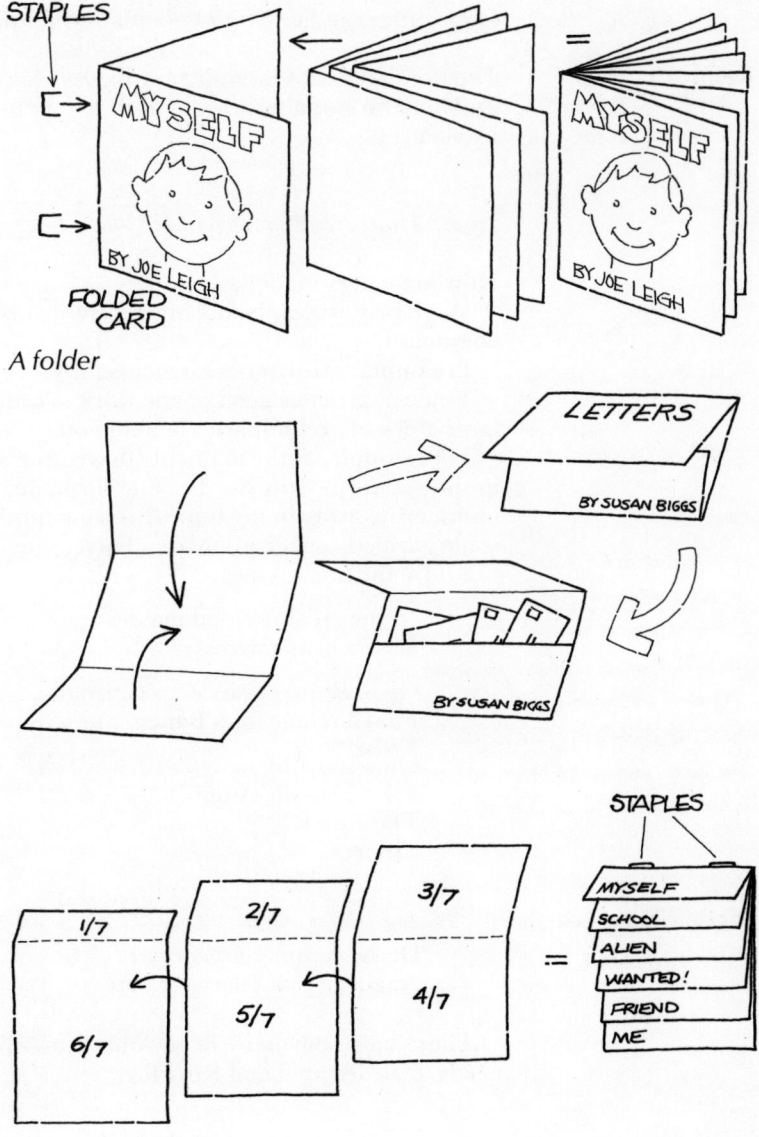

Writer's notebook

Keeping a writer's notebook is a way of catching and preserving ideas which pass through the mind at any time. It makes the most of these fleeting moments of inspiration and provides material when the time is available to write. It encourages you to develop your own personal ideas and to work on them over a longer period. It gives you time to mull over ideas and incubate them.

Plan

You will need a small notebook. Carry it around with you at all times. During the day, as odd phrases, words, ideas flicker through your mind, write them down in case they become useful later; they could grow into poems, stories and essays.

Read

The Russian poet Vladimir Mayakovsky kept such a notebook, and here he explains how he used it to note down ideas he could use later:

from: How Are Verses Made?

How are verses made?
   Work begins long before one receives or is aware of a social command.
   Preliminary work goes on incessantly.
   You can produce good poetic work to order only when you've a large stock of preliminaries behind you.
   For example, at the moment (to write of what has this very minute come into my head) a fine surname, 'Mr Glyceron', is hammering away in my brain, arriving quite by chance out of some garbled conversation about glycerine.
   And some fine rhymes:

> In the creamy cloud masses
> Rose a grim fortress
>
> Go to Rome, France, or Germany,
> Find a refuge for a Bohemian.
>
> On a snorting mare
> I'll ride to the Amur,
> The Amur
> Mourns.

Or:

> Dense summer greenery . . .
> August's rich finery etc., etc.

There's also the metre of an American song I like a lot, which needs to be adapted and Russified:

> Hard-hearted Hannah
> The vamp of Savannah
> The vamp of Savannah
> Gee-ay.

There's the tersely striking alliteration of a poster glimpsed in passing, with the name 'Flora Low':

> Where can I find Flora Low?
> Flora's on the lower floor.

Or, in connection with a synthetic dye factory, called Lyamina's:

> Mummy mixes lovely dye
> 'Cos my mummy's Lyamina.

There are themes of varying clarity and obscurity:
1. Rain in New York.
2. The great theme of the Revolution, which couldn't be done unless you'd lived through it in a village. And so on and so forth.

All these preliminaries are put together in one's head, and the most difficult ones are noted down.

The manner of their future application is all obscure to me, but I know they will be made use of.

All my time goes on these preliminaries. I spend from ten to eighteen hours each day on them, and I'm almost always muttering something or other. My concentration on them accounts for my notorious poetic absent-mindedness.

Work on them goes on with such intensity that in ninety cases out of a hundred I even know the very place where, in all that fifteen years of work, such-and-such a rhyme, alliteration or image came to me and took on its final shape.

> A street.
> I meet ... (The tram from the Sukharev tower to the
>   Sretenka gate, 1913)

> A menacing rain narrowed the eyes,
> While I ... (The Strastnoy monastery, 1912)

> Stroke the shrivelled black cats (Oak tree in Kuntsevo,
>   1914)

> Left
> Left. (Cab on the Embankment, 1917)

> D'Anthèse, son of a bitch. (In the train near Mytishchi,
>   1924)

And so on and so forth.

This 'notebook' is one of the most important preconditions for the composition of the genuine article.

People usually only write about this little book after the poet's death; for years it lies gathering dust, and it's printed posthumously, long after the 'finished' works, but for the writer this book is all-in-all.

Inexperienced poets naturally lack this little book, since they lack practice and experience. Properly worked-out lines are few, and that's why their whole output is anaemic and tedious.

No beginner will, whatever his talents, write something fine straight off; on the other hand, first work is always 'fresher', since it is a vehicle for the stored-up impressions of the time that preceded it.

Only the presence of rigorously thought-out preliminary work gives me the time to finish anything, since my normal output of work in progress is eight to ten lines a day.

A poet regards every meeting, every signpost, every event in whatever circumstances simply as material to be shaped into words.

Once upon a time I embarked on such work as if fearful even to utter words and expressions that seemed to me needful for future poems – I became gloomy, dull and untalkative.

In about 1913, when I was returning from Saratov to Moscow, so as to prove my devotion to a certain female companion, I told her that I was 'not a man, but a cloud in trousers'. When I'd said it, I immediately thought it could be used in a poem; but what if it should at once circulate in conversation and be squandered to no avail? Terribly worried, I put leading questions to the girl for half an hour, and calmed down only when I was quite sure that my words were going in one ear and out the other.

Two years later I needed 'a cloud in trousers' for the title of a whole long poem.

For two days I pondered words to describe the tenderness a lonely man feels for his only love.

How will he cherish and love her?

On the third night I went to bed with a headache, and hadn't thought up anything. During the night the formulation came:

> Your body
> I shall cherish and love
> As a soldier
> Crippled by war
> Useless
> Belonging to no one
> Cherishes his one leg.

I leapt out of bed half-awake. By the dim light of a burnt-down match I wrote on a cigarette packet 'his one leg' and went to sleep. In the morning I puzzled for about two hours over that 'his one leg' written on my cigarette packet; I wondered how it had got there.

A rhyme that has been hooked but not yet landed can poison one's whole existence: you talk without knowing what you're saying, in a daze, you don't sleep, you can almost see that rhyme flying past your eyes.

VLADIMIR MAYAKOVSKY

Write

Many people like playing with words in their mind as they doze – just before drifting off to sleep, for example. Others find walking stimulates their thoughts, but ideas can come at any time. Without a deliberate effort to catch them 'on the wing', they disappear and we forget about them. Carry your notebook and a pencil with you and record anything you observe of interest. Bring it with you to your English lesson and work on the best entries. Once you have started drafting a piece of writing more ideas will come to you which can be recorded in the notebook.

Reading journal

The reading journal helps you to become more sensitive to and critical of what you read. It helps concentration, catches hold of passing perceptions and helps you to reflect more precisely on what you read. The journal is a place to hatch ideas and responses to what you read.

You will need a notebook. Keep it by you as you read. Use it to jot down:

First impressions: What pleases, puzzles or strikes you immediately.

Things that go on in your head as you read: Memories, images which appear, questions which occur to you. Catch these on paper in the form of notes or sketches.

Reflections: Summarise your feelings and judgements at the end of each session or each chapter.

Changing impressions: Reassess characters and events in the light of new information, and look forward, guessing how the book may resolve itself. Predicting and reassessing the story will help you to become an active and intelligent reader.

Your own writing: Writing based on what you read, or stimulated by it. Writing your own stories, poems and experiences will always help you to understand and appreciate those of other people.

The best journal entries:

are short and frequent – rather than long and occasional
are made during reading – rather than afterwards
are tentative – they speculate, question and consider rather than rushing to conclusions
catch responses on the wing – before they slip away or get forgotten
are personal and honest – because only you know what happens in your own head when you read

Extracts from students' reading journals

<u>LORD FOUL'S BANE</u> by Stephen Donaldson (Pages 42 - 131)

Mystified by last scene — too much detail to remember.
Glad to be back with slow-moving events, easy to follow.

<u>Pg 42</u> Biblical language eg 'Behold!' — but sometimes it just
      sounds silly, like Lena saying 'What ill assails you?
      I know not what to do'. Why not 'What's up with
      you? I don't know what to do.' The language is
      getting on my nerves.

The names! Scandanavian sounding: Elric, Loric, Kiril
Threndor, Kevin....KEVIN!!?? That doesn't fit. Even
Berek sounds suspiciously like Derek.

<u>Pg 48-9</u> Lena's description of the land. Map at front
         very useful. Where is the Loresraat?

<u>Having trouble with the family relationships:</u>
Lord Fatherer — Berek Halfhand — first of Old Lords
                        ↓
         Loric Vilesilencer   ┌─────────────────────┐
                        ↓   │ High Lord Damelon   │
         Kevin Landwaster — last stand │ where does <u>he</u> fit in?│
                                      └─────────────────────┘

  <u>Lena's family:</u>   Trell.m. Atiaran
                                    ↓
                          Lena...betrothed(?) Triock

<u>The Stonedown</u> (Pg 63)

    Outside   Inside

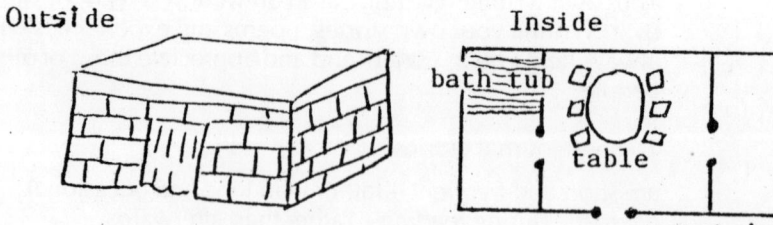

                                        curtained doors

Reflections on 'Soldier, Ask Not' by G.R.Dickins

Whilst reading the story I started to wonder how many drops of water it would take to fill a cup, and counted them; although I didn't get an answer, it proved how lifeless the book was.

All through reading it, I compared it to the original, which I have Read 5 TIMES, and enjoyed each sitting.

Then I realised the story was finishing, because I came to the last few pages or so, and not for any other reason, and with relief I finished in a hurry.

The author doesn't seem to have hit on the right combination to keep it interesting; and I found that it didn't have the same realism as the first book.

Writing down the summary almost put me to sleep, and probably isn't as fluent as the memory I have of the book.

There were minor plots in the book as

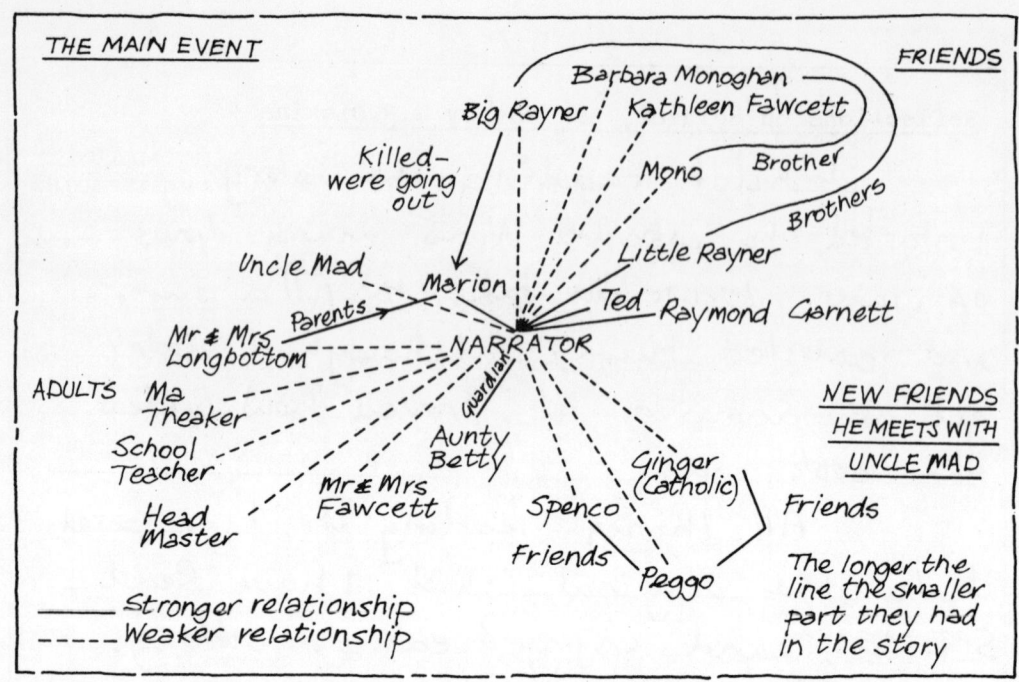

THE MAIN EVENT   FRIENDS

Barbara Monoghan
Kathleen Fawcett
Big Rayner
Mono   Brother
Killed—
were going   Brothers
out
Little Rayner
Uncle Mad   Marion
Ted   Raymond Garnett
Mr & Mrs   Parents
Longbottom ------ NARRATOR

ADULTS Ma   NEW FRIENDS
Theaker   HE MEETS WITH
School   UNCLE MAD
Teacher   Aunty
Betty   Ginger
Mr & Mrs   (Catholic)   Friends
Head   Fawcett   Spenco
Master   The longer the
Friends   Peggo   line the smaller
part they had
——— Stronger relationship   in the story
- - - Weaker relationship

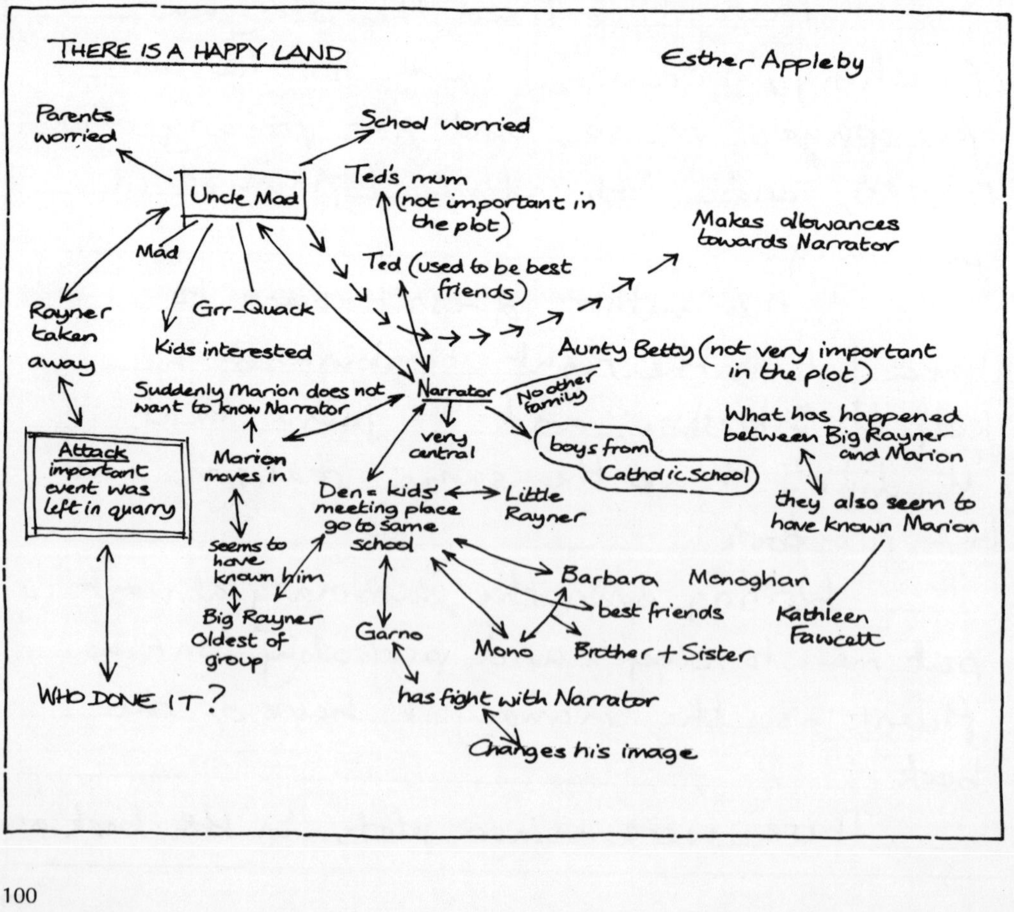

THERE IS A HAPPY LAND   Esther Appleby

Parents   School worried
worried
Ted's mum
Uncle Mad   (not important in   Makes allowances
the plot)   towards Narrator
Mad   Ted (used to be best
Rayner   Grr-Quack   friends)
taken   Aunty Betty (not very important
away   Kids interested   in the plot)
Suddenly Marion does not
want to know Narrator   Narrator   No other
family   What has happened
Attack   very   between Big Rayner
important   Marion   central   boys from   and Marion
event was   moves in   Catholic School
left in quarry   Den = kids' Little   they also seem to
seems to   meeting place Rayner   have known Marion
have   go to same
known him   school   Barbara   Monoghan
Big Rayner   best friends   Kathleen
Oldest of   Garno   Fawcett
group   Mono   Brother + Sister
WHO DONE IT?   has fight with Narrator

Changes his image

Critical diary

Keeping any style of diary helps the writer to reflect on experience. Sometimes when you start writing, unexpected ideas will occur to you and will reshape your views. We see the critical diary as a way of developing your own independent critical views.

We all enjoy expressing our opinions about the people and events around us. If you receive a newspaper, especially a Sunday paper, you will know that reviews and previews of television programmes, plays, books, films and shows are very popular.

Write

You will need a small notebook in which you will write each day. Some of the things you might like to write about are:
- books
- stories you hear
- television programmes
- current affairs
- assemblies
- poetry you have read
- newspaper articles
- an interesting discussion
- a film
- a lesson that starts you thinking
- pictures
- photographs
- advertisements that catch your attention
- music you hear

Read

On pages 102 and 103 are some extracts from the critical diary of a fifteen-year-old girl, Emma:

FEBRUARY.
7th - MONDAY.

I broadened my horizons today, educating myself in the lunchhour, rather than arguing with the dinner ladies, by attending a lunchtime poetry reading session.

Sue Hackman and Pete Dougill sat in front of pupils and teachers reading the selected poems. They ranged from William Carlos - Williams' description of cold plums, to a rather shocking twentieth century rape.

They were well read, and lightly discussed afterwards. We were told why various ones were chosen, and a little about them. One or two of the poems were too deep to appreciate in such a small space of time but most were lyrical and pleasant to listen to. The atmosphere was relaxed, and the idea appealed to me a great deal.

The audience was small which

FEBRUARY
10ᵗʰ - Thursday.

The name 'Roger M°Gough' had been whispered around school all week. People bought the tickets and the whole of Imberhome became decorated with poetry for the special poem week. Today the hero actually would come to our school and read his poetry. I had been ill all night, and spent a day of recovery in bed. Gaining some strength by the afternoon I ventured into school to watch him.

It was quite exciting, seeing someone in the flesh whose books you have read and whose poems you have laughed at. He was not a stunning superstar, but a rather tatty looking, middle aged man with glasses.

He began to read his poetry. The words were spoken rather too quickly and I found myself almost straining to depict sentences, yet I managed to

Personal research

This activity encourages you to use writing as a tool for investigation. Often we write only to pass on information or prove our knowledge to other people. Here, you can use writing as a way of following up ideas that interest you. You are the audience. Write for yourself.

Pick a subject in which you have a genuine interest and about which you need to find out more. Avoid choosing favourite but well-worn projects about which you are already well informed. Some students find it useful to put the title in the form of a question, so that they have a sense of purpose and direction.

Here are some titles students have chosen in the past:
- *How my great grandmother lived*
- *What will I need to consider as I prepare to leave home and live independently?*
- *What should I bear in mind when I buy my first car?*
- *How does my baby brother learn to do things like walking and talking?*

1   Get a loose-leaf folder and divide it into three sections: 'notes and sketches', 'diary' and 'presentation'.

2   Start off by deciding on three or four things you need to know. Leave reference books till last. Don't be satisfied with getting your information second-hand. Go and find it from the places themselves and the people who know.
- Tape an interview with someone who has relevant experience or knowledge.
- Ask friends and family if they have any knowledge or acquaintances who might help you.
- Write to specialist organisations, clubs, companies or people who could help.
- Make a visit to somewhere of significance to your research.

3 Keep tape recordings, sketches and notes as you go along. Jot down any ideas and questions that occur to you as you progress. Do not worry at this stage about copying and storing vast numbers of facts. Do not concern yourself about writing in full sentences. A list of key ideas, a star chart, flow diagram or labelled sketch will be enough to prompt your memory later. Be content to get to grips with your subject. Keep your jottings in the 'notes and sketches' file section.

4 At the end of each session, write into the project diary what you have done that day. Say what you have found that has interested, puzzled or impressed you. Mention any problems you have encountered and ideas for future activities.

This diary should be kept in the special section of your file. Although it is not for marking, it will be read by your teacher, as a way of following your progress. Your teacher might be able to make suggestions.

5 Finally, keep one or two sessions to write a brief introduction to your subject, written for someone who is interested but not an expert. This section of your work should be clearly and carefully presented, as it will be read by other people. It need not be too detailed: sort out for your reader those aspects of the subject that are of general interest. Write it up in the 'presentation' section.